# SERIAL KILLERS

igloobooks

*Published in 2017*
*by Igloo Books Ltd*
*Cottage Farm*
*Sywell*
*NN6 0BJ*
*www.igloobooks.com*

*Copyright © 2017 Igloo Books Ltd*

*HUN001 0817*
*2 4 6 8 10 9 7 5 3 1*
*ISBN 978-1-78810-113-4*

*Written by Lauren A Forry and Deborah Llewelyn*

*Printed and manufactured in China*

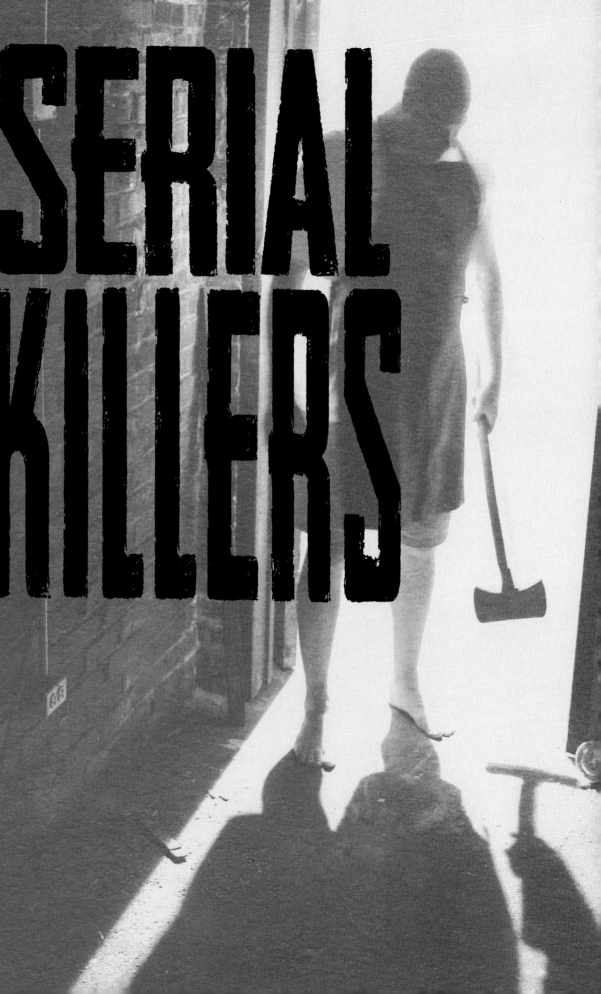

# SERIAL KILLERS

# Contents

# Introduction

No matter how angry they might become, most people know how to stop themselves from using aggressive behaviour or extreme violence towards others.

- - - - - - - - - - - - - - - - - - - - - - - - - - - - - - - - - - - - - - - - - - - - - - - - - -

**Even in frightening situations, there just isn't the urge to kill someone and relationships are a crucial and key part of life. Having a moral sense of right and wrong is there for most of us. There's a safety catch that gives us control over our impulses and, just as importantly, we feel empathy for others.**

For serial killers, right and wrong, control over violent behaviour and anger, and a moral code seem not to exist while urges are extremely strong and the ability to act them out comes with a complete lack of understanding or empathy for their victims. There are simply no feelings, except perhaps anger, or attachment to those that are tortured, raped, sexually abused and killed, even for child victims.

The term serial killer was coined in 1971 but, as far back as the 1400s, there were those who subjected their victims to the most terrifying ordeals. Gilles de Rais, a French nobleman, is probably the first documented serial killer, who was convicted of torturing, raping and murdering hundreds of young children – particularly boys – in the 15th century. These vulnerable victims were lured to his residences where they were mutilated while de Rais ejaculated over his dying victims.

Wolf men in the 16th century were sexual predators who committed senseless murders against victims, first subjecting them to sexual attacks. The problem was widespread and, according to some experts, Lycanthropy – as it was termed – was one of the most pressing social concerns of the day. Frenchman Gilles Garnier and Peter Stubbe from Germany were both sexual predators of children, who ripped their victims apart before cannibalising them. Stubbe even mutilated his own son and ate his brain. Wolf men continued their practices throughout each century from the 1500s onwards. Albert Fish, the American cannibal serial killer, active in the early 20th century, was dubbed the "Werewolf of Wisteria", and was known to dance naked when there was a full moon. Ed Gein was another killer who is cited as dancing under the moon, wearing the woman suit he was making for himself following his own trauma at the death of his mother. When Gein was suspected of the murder of a local tradeswoman, police found the suit made from the skin of the killer's victims. However, other serial killers view themselves differently to wolf men and lunatics. Dennis Nilsen wondered if he was completely evil.

*LEFT: Judge Larry Gram standing at podium in front of the bench in his courtroom, speaking to the reporters and cameramen surrounding him at press conference after sentencing serial killer Jeffrey Dahmer*

According to statistics, the average serial killer is a white male from a low to middle class background, aged in his 20s or 30s. Many of these killers have been emotionally and/or physically and sexually abused by their parents; a large number were adopted as babies or young children; and most began their criminal activities by torturing animals and setting fires. Serial killers are also known to be fairly prolific at wetting the bed as older children and, together with cruelty to animals and arson, give rise to what's known as the "triad" of symptoms. These are considered today as "red-flag" behaviours. Most serial killers experienced extreme trauma as small children, or suffered from brain injury in some way, and a large number of these murderers are fascinated by authority and the police; Ted Bundy and John Gacy both impersonated a police officer at times in order to gain the trust of their victims.

With psychopathic natures, serial killers do not understand how to have relationships in the way that most people do. They have no sympathy or empathy for those around them, but learn how to act appropriately in order not to bring undue attention to themselves, by closely observing others. This is then used manipulatively to entice others to trust them so that their fantasies – often developed since childhood – can be enacted. Some experts cite that serial killers are extremely good actors, and Henry Lee Lucas actually said: "... being like a movie star ... you're just playing the part". While Ted Bundy was known to use various disguises, John Gacy did a great deal of work for charity and dressed as a clown to entertain adults and children alike at charitable events, while the unknown Zodiac Killer chose to dress like an executioner.

In the US, the FBI consider two or more murders, committed at different times, the work of a serial killer. However, others define them as having murdered three or more people. A large number of serial killers have some form of sexual contact with their victims – providing them with most of the criteria associated with being this type of criminal – where anger, thrills, attention seeking, extreme violence and sexual gratification are all key. Others go further and have sexual intercourse with the corpses of their victims, while mutilation, dismemberment and cannibalism are not uncommon. However, there are those with a different type of mental stability who murder their victims for attention alone including the likes of former nurse Beverley Allitt., or those like Zhou Kehua whose only motive was robbery.

Some serial killers, like Robert Black, refuse to talk about some of the victims they are suspected of killing, while others are willing to divulge as much detail as possible once they are caught. Serial killers often cite that they would not have stopped killing had they not been brought to justice. Others have various excuses for their murderous acts, including Jeffrey Dahmer, who said that a "part" of him was missing. Bundy was known to have strongly believed that violent pornography was to blame, while a number of others – including Gacy and Alexander Spesivtsev – said that their victims deserved to die and that they were ridding the world of undesirables.

Serial killers are rational and calculating, even though most have a less than average IQ, with a sadistic need to dominate their victims and a psychological motive for murdering them. They are incredibly adept at "blending" in to society and are more likely to be the polite, well-spoken and well dressed individual trying to entice you to trust them than the unwashed homeless person ranting away to an imaginary companion. They have cleverly developed their methods, and have evolved, like all predators, stalking their victims, luring them with promises before uncontrollable urges lead to terror and ultimately death.

ABOVE: Some serial killers feel a sense of injustice at the way they have been portrayed in the press. This is David "Son of Sam" Berkowitz's letter to "Daily News" reporter and columnist Jimmy Breslin

# L'ILLUSTRÉ

## DU PETIT JOURNAL

TOUS LES
DIMANCHES

ET SON SUPPLÉMENT AGRICOLE
GRAND HEBDOMADAIRE POUR TOUS

50c
12-3-33

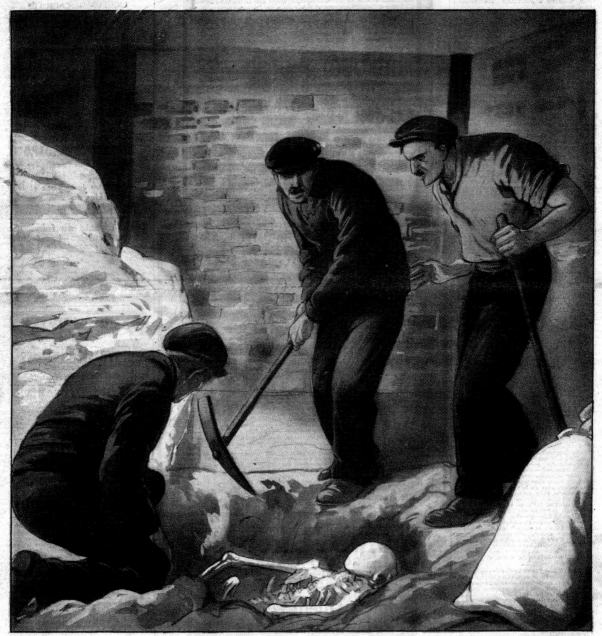

## UNE VICTIME DE LANDRU ?

Le sinistre souvenir de l'homme de Gambais et le secret de sa tragique affaire viennent d'être évoqués. Un squelette a été découvert à Clichy, enseveli sous les fondations d'un immeuble de la rue de Paris, voisin de celui où habita Landru. Cette coïncidence a ému l'opinion. Ces restes seraient-ils ceux d'une victime de Landru ? C'est peu probable. Mais, cependant, quel est ce squelette mystérieux ?                    (Voir l'article page 3).

*ABOVE: A French newspaper covers the discovery of a dead body,*
*buried in the foundations of a building, on the Rue de Paris in Clichy,*
*close to where serial killer Henri Desire Landru used to live*

# Male
# Killers

----------------------------------------

# Stephen Griffiths

On 22ⁿᵈ June 2009, 43-year-old Susan Rushworth disappeared in Bradford, West Yorkshire. Shelley Armitage, 31, disappeared on 26ᵗʰ April 2010, followed by Suzanne Blamires, 36, in May 2010.

- - - - - - - - - - - - - - - - - - - - - - - - - - - - - - - - - - - - - - - - - - - - - -

**Stephen Griffiths, aged 40 at the time of his arrest for the three murders in May 2010, had been living in Bradford for a little over a decade, where he was studying for a PhD in Criminology at Bradford University.**

He was extremely interested in the criminal history of Kenneth Valentine, a local man who had killed twice, in the same block of flats where Griffiths was living. Valentine's first victim was a sex worker and Griffiths beat him badly for the murder. But, it is cited that the two men were so close that some thought them to be lovers.

Valentine had rented out a room in his flat to working girls who paid him £5 each time they brought a punter back. What they didn't know was that he had drilled a tiny spy hole through the wall so he could watch the women. Caroline Creevy, 25, was killed in Valentine's flat in 1996 when she did discover his secret. Valentine was caught on CCTV disposing of Caroline's body and was convicted of her murder in 1998.

Despite his horror at what Valentine had done, just over 10 years later, Griffiths was to become a triple murderer. The former public schoolboy had befriended many of the sex workers in the run-down area of Bradford where he lived. He had let them stay at his flat, cooked them meals and even done their washing, but his arrest at the age of 17 for an unprovoked knife attack on a man, for which he served three years, meant that police were suspicious of Griffiths. He had even said in custody that he wanted to become a murderer – psychiatrists warned he was obsessed with serial killers – and police had been watching him prior to the murders he committed for a couple of years and had even confiscated his hunting weapons.

Griffiths was obsessed with crime films and had a bizarre website on which he even admitted he was going to kill. Susan Rushworth was only linked to Griffiths by a tiny speck of blood found in his bath. It is reported that he dismembered all three women in the bathroom of his flat. Shelley Armitage and her boyfriend both had an addiction to heroin and Shelley worked on the streets to feed their habit. She also had a number of enemies, but her disappearance was extremely upsetting for her closest friend Suzanne Blamires. Suzanne also had a drug habit, which had turned her from a middle-class achiever into a woman working the streets. It was Suzanne's murder that would lead police to Griffiths.

CCTV showed Suzanne fleeing from his flat before he punched her and knocked her unconscious. He then shot her twice in the head with a crossbow. Video footage and body parts found after his arrest confirmed that Griffiths had killed, skinned and then eaten his victims.

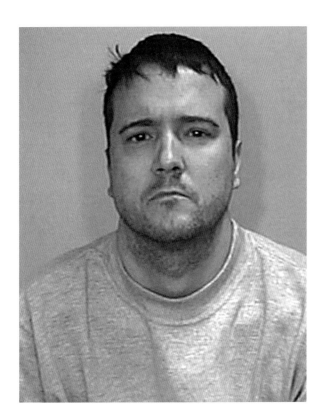

*LEFT: Stephen Griffiths, the "Crossbow Cannibal"*

ABOVE: Some of the crossbows
used by Stephen Griffiths

BELOW: Police continue their fingertip forensic search
outside the home of Stephen Griffiths in May 2010

# Marcos Antunes Trigueiro

Marcos Antunes Trigueiro is a known Brazilian murderer and rapist born in Brasilia de Minas.

**Born in 1978, he spent some of his early life in São Paulo and Rio De Janeiro, settling again in Minas Gerais in his later life. Trigueiro's younger life saw happier times, when he was twice married and he fathered five children. It was not until April 2009 that Marcos took a twisted turn and began his cruel journey into sexual assault and murder.**

Trigueiro's modus operandi followed a distinct pattern. His victims were kidnapped, three were raped and all five died from strangulation using items available to him in the immediate vicinity. The mobile phones of the victims were always missing from the crime scene. One of the victims was strangled with her necklace, and another suffered the cruel fate of being strangled by the seatbelt in her car. His first victim, Ana Carolina Menezes Assunção, was found strangled to death by a shoelace in the back of her car. Ana had been molested then killed, and her fourteen-month baby was found lying on the seat next to her lifeless body. The baby was apparently unharmed.

Another of Trigueiro's victims was Natalia Cristina de Almeida Paiva, who was reported missing on the 27th January 2009. Her car was found abandoned in the Camargos neighbourhood and her body a week later in Sarzedo, over 100 km from where her vehicle was discovered. Natalia had been strangled to death.

Under forensic analysis it was discovered that Trigueiro's first three victims showed evidence of semen traces, all of which shared the same DNA. It wasn't until February 2010 that civil police of Minas Gerais arrested Trigueiro on suspicion of murder when they had traced the mobile phones of the victims. Four of the five mobile devices were found in his possession, while the fifth phone was found in the possession of his wife, linking him directly to each victim.

During police interviews, Trigueiro confessed to all of the murders, and DNA matching to the semen traces found on the earlier victims gave solid evidence that he was responsible for their deaths.

Trigueiro was tried and convicted of three of the five murders and was sentenced to more than 100 years in prison.

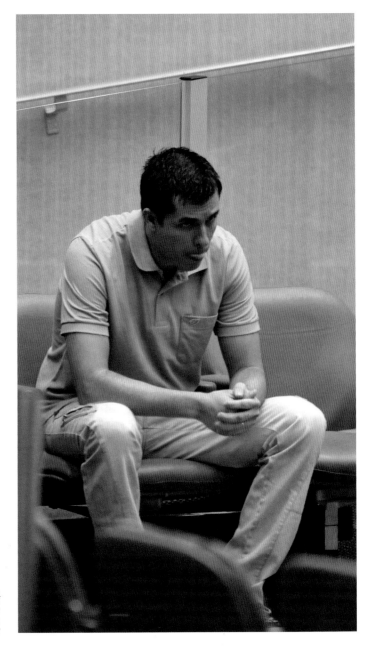

*RIGHT: Marcos Antunes Trigueiro, best known as "The Maniac of Contagem", during his trial at Forum Lafayete in June 2010 in Belo Horizonte, Brazil*

# Jack Mogale

Serial rapist and killer Jack Mogale was linked by police to the brutal attack and rape of a teenager to whom he had offered a lift in his car while posing as a Zion Christian Church preacher and prophet.

---

**Rather than taking the girl where she needed to go, he drove her to a veld, or veldt (a rural wide open space in South Africa), where he repeatedly assaulted her until she was unconscious. As the young woman lost consciousness, Mogale then raped her.**

It was the girl's cell phone, found in his shack, along with her underwear and sangoma beads that he wore at the time of the attack, that eventually linked him to the crime. The brutal and sexual assault on the girl was similar to a number of attacks on local women in the Westonaria area and police realised they were dealing with the same attacker. They began looking for a ZCC preacher, wearing sangoma beads, driving a white VW Golf. When police later searched the veld outside Westonaria, it was here that the decomposing bodies of most of his victims were found. He was charged with 16 counts of murder, the rape of 19 women and for the kidnapping of 18 victims.

Born in 1968, Mogale began his killing spree in 2008 and, on his arrest, made a statement to police confessing to seven of the cases against him. But, following his statement, he became emotional and told South African Brigadier Piet Byleveld – also instrumental in bringing Cedric Maake to justice – that he lost control when he was with women and had no idea what he was doing. He said: "I would kill all of them if they do not give me what I want". He initialled the first page of his statement but refused to sign the rest of it.

When he was arrested at his shack in Zuurbekom, South Africa, on 27th March 2009, Mogale tried to urinate on police officers even though his wrists were handcuffed in front of him. He took out his penis and swore at members of the public who had gathered to see what was going on.

At his trial in 2010, one of his victims, by then 20 years old, told the South Gauteng High Court how she was beaten unconscious by Mogale with a brick and woke 24 hours later to discover that she had been raped and sodomised. She had met the killer for the first time on 13th March 2008 in Venterspost when he offered her a lift. There were two small children and a woman, a neighbour, in the car and the victim felt she would be safe. Mogale dropped the woman and toddlers off in another part of Venterspost before setting off for the shops in Westonaria with the young woman.

Realising she was in great danger as the VW Golf arrived at the veld and she was forced out of the car, the woman tried to hit Mogale with a brick as he started strangling her. She asked her attacker if he wanted to rape her and he replied by asking if men had told her that her vagina was nice. While he strangled the woman with one hand,

Mogale grabbed the brick and continued to hit the woman over the head until she lost consciousness. She awoke from her attack and managed to summon help from a security guard at nearby buildings who called an ambulance. Medical examination found that she had been badly assaulted, raped and sodomised by her attacker and was suffering from serious head, face and body injuries. Mogale had left her for dead with a fractured jaw that required reconstructive surgery and she lost several teeth. In another case against Mogale, a mother and her toddler were both killed.

At his trial, the witness and neighbour described how Mogale had lured the teenage victim into his car after his attempt to kidnap her and her children had failed. Mary Sepeng was in the car with her two toddlers when Mogale picked up the young woman. Like the victim, Mary hadn't met Mogale before and she believed his story about being a ZCC preacher. He had tried to drive down a gravel road towards a veld in Venterspost, despite the two children in the back, but had changed his mind when he spotted traffic police on a main road.

After picking up the young woman and dropping Mary at her home address, even though as far as she was aware, Mogale had never been there before, she took down the registration of his car. Only two of his victims survived their brutal attacks and Mogale was sentenced to 16 life sentences, a further 23 years and no possibility of parole.

*ABOVE: The South African veld is a large, remote expanse that Jack Mogale utilised to the full when committing his crimes*

# Steve Wright

Steve Wright, often referred to as the "Suffolk Strangler", was responsible for the murders of five women in Ipswich in 2006.

-------------------------------------------------------------------------------------------

**Wright was born in 1958 and was one of four children. His mother left when Wright was eight and his father, a military policeman, remarried. Wright was married and divorced twice and had two children, one with each of his former wives.**

He became known for his addictive gambling habits, heavy drinking and his propensity for domestic violence but, in the mid 1990s and again in 2000, Wright attempted suicide, once by carbon monoxide poisoning in his car and the second time by taking an overdose of pills.

In 2001, he was convicted of theft when he stole £100 to pay off gambling debts. It is also known that Wright worked on a cruise ship at the same time as Suzy Lamplugh in the 1980s before the London estate agent simply disappeared after meeting a client at a house in Fulham. There has never been any evidence to link Wright to the disappearance and murder of 25-year-old Suzy.

In late 2006, five prostitutes were found dead at different locations over a six-week period. The women were discovered in the surrounding countryside, stripped naked and, in two instances, posed in a cruciform position. Despite their bodies being stripped naked by the killer, the women had not been sexually assaulted before their deaths.

Wright attempted to dispose of any evidence that would lead to his capture by ensuring his car and clothes were scrupulously cleaned after each attack. However, traces of Wright's DNA were discovered on three of the victims's bodies and microscopic fibres found on all five women were linked to his clothing, car and home.

The police sifted through 10,000 hours of CCTV footage of the red light district and surrounding area of Ipswich and, by using an automatic car registration plate reader, they were able to identify a Ford Mondeo in the area at the time at which each of the women disappeared.

On 19th December 2006, Suffolk Police arrested Steve Wright on suspicion of murder. The trial, which lasted for six weeks, resulted in a conviction for all five murders and a sentence of life imprisonment with a recommendation that he is never released from prison.

*LEFT: A police van carrying Steve Wright (right, under blanket) leaves Ipswich Magistrates Court in December 2006*

*OPPOSITE: A police officer stands outside the house of Steve Wright during the investigation into the murders of five prostitutes in the Ipswich area*

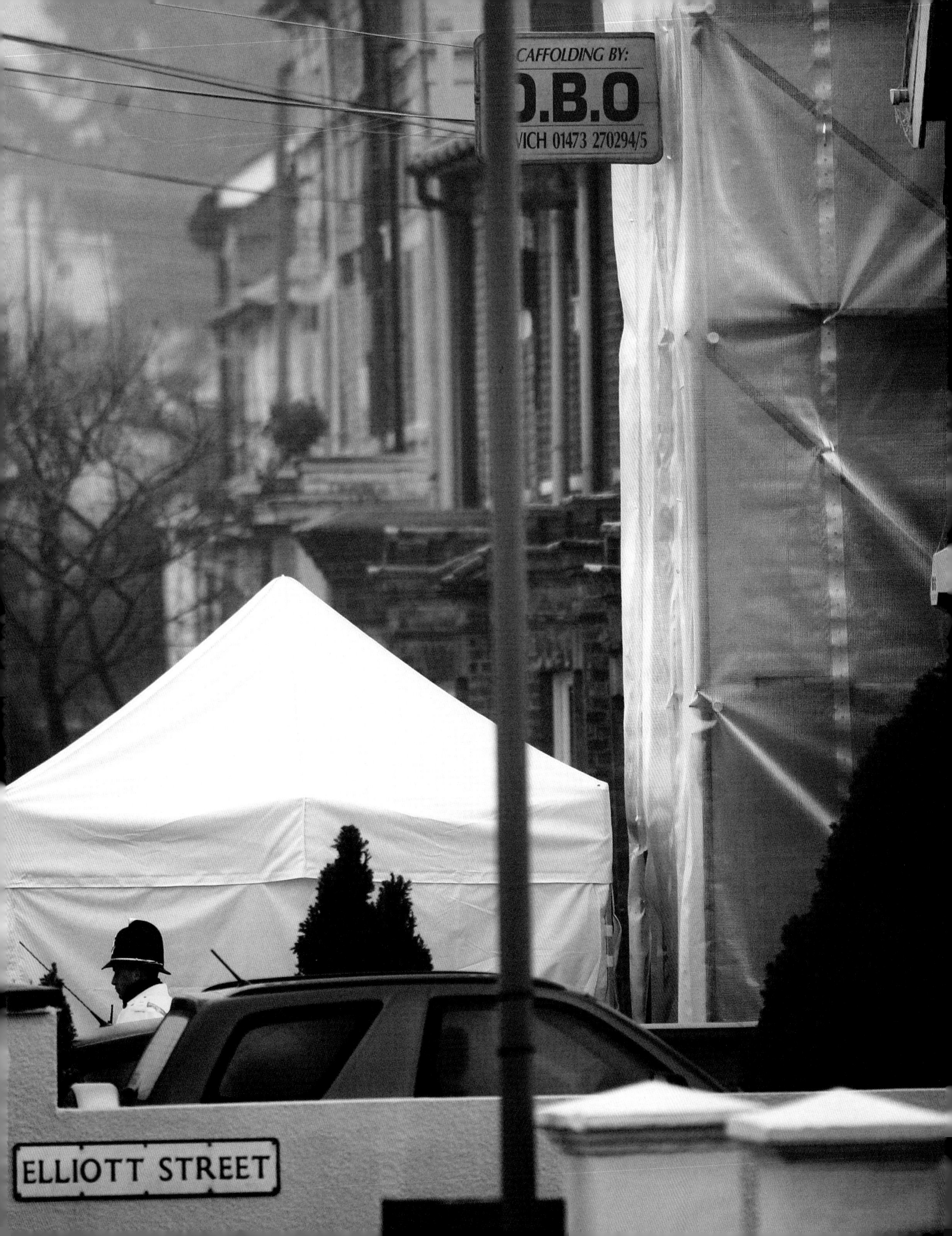
01473 270294/5
ELLIOTT STREET

# Very Idham Henyansyah

In 2008, Indonesian serial killer, Very Idham Henyansah confessed to murdering 11 people following his arrest. In 2013, he was still awaiting execution at Kesambi Penitentiary in Cirebon.

- - - - - - - - - - - - - - - - - - - - - - - - - - - - - - - - - - - - - -

**Born in 1978, Henyansyah was particularly brutal in his treatment of his victims. A number of bodies were found buried in the garden of his home in East Java, but the remains of one of his victims was found cut into pieces and skewered on a crowbar by the side of a road in Jakarta.**

Many of Henyansyah's victims were homosexual men, who were murdered between 2006 and 2008. Described as sadistic and possibly insane, he was found guilty of murdering and dismembering Hery Santoso who offered to pay Henyansyah if allowed to have sex with the crazed man's boyfriend. He also confessed to the murder of another 10 victims including a mother and her three-year-old daughter.

Others cite that Henyansyah was certainly not insane at the time of the killings and that he was well aware of the crimes he was committing. While it is known that Henyansyah felt some fear following each killing, when he remained undetected, he continued to search for new victims.

Henyansyah was born in the agricultural region of Jombang, where religious beliefs are often strong. At the age of 10, he began displaying signs of mental instability and grew increasingly violent. His earlier victims, while still living close to his hometown, were all attacked in a short space of time, following the break up of a relationship with another young man who went on to marry a local girl. Henyansyah was diagnosed as a sociopath with anti-social personality disorder. He had never got on well with either his parents or his siblings and Henyansyah has indicated he thinks he is "special" and has shown signs of narcissistic personality disorder.

He was nicknamed the "Singing Serial Killer" for his singing both in court and in prison. Also known as Ryan, Henyansyah published his autobiography in 2009 and, the following year, married convicted drug dealer Eny Wijaya in order to fulfill his mother's wish that he marry a woman. Although it was reported that Henyansyah's death sentence would be appealed, should that fail he would undoubtedly face the firing squad.

*RIGHT: Self-confessed Indonesian serial killer Very Idham Henyansyah waves behind bars after a district court in Depok handed out his death sentence*

# Petr Zelenka

Petr Zelenka became known as "The Heparin Killer" when he was found guilty of murdering seven patients in his care in 2006.

**Zelenka was a nurse at a hospital in Havlickud Brod in the Czech Republic and targeted both male and female patients. His modus operandi was to administer large doses of the blood-thinning drug heparin which, when given in sizeable amounts, causes severe internal bleeding. Zelenka had no authority to administer the drug without supervision from a doctor, which obviously he never sought.**

Zelenka – born on 27th February 1976 – attempted to kill a total of 17 patients during his murdering stint between May 2006 and September 2006 at the hospital and succeeded in killing seven elderly men and women. He kept vials of heparin hidden away and would inject the drug directly into the veins of his victims.

The hospital first became suspicious when an unusually high number of patients were dying from internal bleeding. Management at the hospital negotiated with Zelenka to leave his position in September 2006 and the police were informed of the suspicious deaths that had occurred. Following an investigation, Zelenka was arrested on 1st December 2006 and he confessed to the murders. His lawyer was quoted to have said that Zelenka killed on impulse, targeting the weak and the elderly as a means to "test" doctors. He believed that they were not knowledgeable enough to identify that the patients had actually been murdered.

On 22nd February 2008, Judge Vacek sentenced Zelenka to life imprisonment in a maximum-security hospital. His lawyer pleaded for a lesser sentence on the grounds of diminished responsibility, claiming that his client was mentally ill, but the court rejected the plea. Judge Vacek indicated Zelenka's crimes deserved the death penalty but, since it was abolished in 1990, a life sentence – with no possible parole for 20 years – was the only viable option.

*LEFT: Flanked by security personnel, Petr Zelenka reacts during the verdict at the courtroom in Hradec Kralove city*

# Stephen Port

On 23rd November 2016, British chef, Stephen Port, was convicted of 11 assaults including the drugging, raping and murdering of four young homosexuals.

---

**In November 2016, Port was found guilty of the murder of Anthony Walgate, a 23-year-old student from Hull; Gabriel Kovari, 22, from Slovakia; Daniel Whitworth, 21, a chef from Kent; and Jack Taylor, 25, a forklift driver from Dagenham. The enquiry found that Port drugged and raped them, using the date-rape drug GHB, alongside a cocktail of other drugs.**

Born in Southend-on-Sea, Port was raised by his parents in Dagenham and lived most of his adolescent life in quiet solitude. Those who knew him – including his neighbour, Ryan – described him as being a private man with child-like tendencies. During his young adult life, he lived independently in a flat in Barking and worked as a chef at the Stagecoach bus depot in West Ham.

Although each murder case had striking similarities, the investigation failed to link the deaths at the time. As a result of this, Port continued to commit crime in his community, while the previous murders remained unsolved.

Port met each of his victims via online social networks and the dating app Grindr. His first victim was a young fashion student, Anthony Walgate, who worked as an escort alongside his studies. Port contacted Walgate via the website 'Sleepyboys' and pretended to be a client. He offered him £800 for his services. On the morning following the murder of Walgate, Port contacted the emergency services to report the young man he'd dumped outside his flat, claiming he appeared to have "collapsed or had had a seizure or was drunk". Evidence failed to link Port to Walgate's death. Port was later convicted of perverting the course of justice in relation to Walgate's death, as his account of the death was inconsistent. He was sentenced to just eight months imprisonment.

Two months after the death of Walgate, Port claimed the lives of Kovari and Whitworth. The murders were carried out within a two-week period in August and September 2014. Their bodies were dumped in St Margaret's graveyard near his flat in Barking. Port planted a fake suicide note with the body of Whitworth that claimed he was responsible for the death of Kovari and that he killed himself out of guilt. Kovari's death was treated as "unexplained", but later a post-mortem examination found he had died from a mixed drug overdose. Following the murder of Kovari and Whitworth, Port was imprisoned from March-June 2015, serving just half of his proposed eight-month sentence. The final victim in Port's string of murders was Jack Taylor. Taylor was killed three months after Port was released from prison, in September 2015. His body was found near the same graveyard.

Despite the fact that all four victims were found in similar locations and all identified as young homosexuals, the police failed to link the murders or issue any warnings with local LGBT communities. Although the detail of each murder case differed slightly, Port's method of administering a deadly overdose before raping the victims and dumping their bodies remained the same.

Each fatal case obtained striking similarities. Port initiated the contact via social media and he then set up a date at a bar or club, drugged the victims and lured them to his flat in Barking where he would penetrate them while unconscious. Following this, he would dispose the bodies in close proximity to his home; this was always carried out in a vile, undignified manner. In one instance he dragged the body out into the street in front of his flat, an act both shocking and careless. It was as if he wanted to be caught. Despite the strong resemblances linking each murder, the police were quick to assume the death of Whitworth was a suicidal act, as the note suggested. The inquests into the deaths highlighted a number of other flaws, including various objects related to each crime that the police had not tested or forensically analysed.

As a result of questions about the effectiveness of the police investigation into the murders and victims involved, the Independent Police Complaints Commission (IPCC) were ordered to investigate whether the police officers involved in the case should be held accountable for their inability to link the four cases and involve sufficient witnesses in the cases.

On 25th November 2016, at the Old Bailey, Port was found guilty of 11 separate counts. He was sentenced to life imprisonment and a whole life order, which means he is not eligible for parole and is unlikely to be released from prison.

*OPPOSITE: Family of victim, Jack Taylor, speak to the media after a guilty verdict being found against Stephen Port at Old Bailey in November 2016*

# Thozamile Taki

Thozamile Taki became widely known as the "Sugar cane Killer" after he murdered 13 women and dumped their bodies in agricultural plantations in South Africa.

**His victims were aged between 18 and 25 years old and he lured the women by offering them jobs at various companies. His deceitful promises gained their trust so he was able to arrange a meeting with them, on the pretence that they needed to bring money as a bribe to secure employment.**

Once they were in a secluded location, he robbed them of their mobile phone, bank cards and money, and raped them before strangling them and discarding their bodies. Eleven victims were found in the sugar cane plantations of Umzinto and two victims were discovered in the tea plantations outside Port St. Johns.

Their bodies were found partially decomposed and it was suspected that several body parts had been provided to a local traditional healer. Provincial police set up a specialist team to identify and capture the murderer.

Taki was arrested in September 2007 when he was suspected of the crimes. He was remanded at Westville Prison during the trial, where he attempted an escape along with eight other inmates. Taki fell from the roof of his fourth floor cell and sustained serious injuries while the other prisoners managed to escape. The trial was adjourned until he had recovered from his injuries.

On 2nd March 2010, he entered the court in a wheelchair as a result of his fall three years previously, where more than 100 people testified against Taki while there was substantial evidence that the killer was using his victims's mobile phones after their disappearances.

Judge King Ndlovu described Taki to be "a jackal in sheep's hide", and sentenced him on the 19th January 2011 to 13 life sentences for the murders and 208 years for armed robbery.

*RIGHT: South Africa's "Sugar cane Killer" Thozamile Taki at the KwaZulu-Natal High Court in Durban in January 2011*

# David Randitsheni

In August 2009, David Randitsheni, then aged 45, committed suicide in Thohoyandou prison, South Africa.

**At the date of his suicide, Randitsheni had served just three weeks of his 16 life sentences and 220 years, having been convicted of 10 counts of murder, 17 counts of rape, indecent assault and 18 kidnappings. All his victims, except one woman, were children.**

Randitsheni's killing and serial raping began in 2004 before he was finally identified through DNA analysis in 2008. Eight of his victims were found murdered in Modimolle's Phagameng village, where people were terrorised by the abuse, torture, rape and killings of these children. Once he was sentenced, many organisations backed the Magistrate Court Judge's ruling and claimed that a strong message was being sent to all perpetrators who thought it acceptable that girls, and women in South Africa generally, could suffer a truly barbaric death at the hands of monsters like Randitsheni.

Child and baby rape in South Africa has long been in existence and the country has some of the highest incidences in the world. In 2000, more than 67,000 cases of rape and sexual assaults against children were reported, a rise of more than 40% since 1998 where, worryingly, children under seven years old suffered the largest increase in attacks. Baby gang rape is also particularly prevalent in South Africa and, in some cases, the child victims are attacked by members of their own family.

Randitsheni was arrested in Lwamodo village near Venda after being positively linked to 17 cases of rape, murder and indecent assault and co-operated with the investigation, although he pleaded not guilty at his trial. It would lead to the fastest serial murder and rape trial in South African history with a conviction and sentence achieved in two days. He had attacked 17 girls, one boy and one woman which led to the largest mass DNA screening South Africa had ever seen where 543 samples were tested, providing a positive match to Randitsheni. Investigators first found two bodies – one that had decomposed and another that was a relatively recent victim. The township DNA samples revealed that one of the victims lived close to the killer, who had a wife and three children. Police had hoped that like other serial killers, the man they sought lived in the small township and operated close to home. Once the initial two bodies were found, a task team was set up to search for the serial killer, where more bodies were discovered and more rapes uncovered. Although 113 witnesses were lined up, the testimonies of the first three helped to put Randitsheni behind bars – no others were even called to court.

Judge Roger Claassen of Modimolle Circuit High Court declared that Randitsheni would not be eligible for parole for 35 years, at the age of 80. However, he was found hanged in his cell just weeks after the trial.

RIGHT: Modimolle was the hunting ground of South African serial killer David Randitsheni

# Yoo Young-Chul

Yoo Young-Chul was a methodical serial killer and self-confessed cannibal born in South Korea on 18<sup>th</sup> April 1970.

- - - - - - - - - - - - - - - - - - - - - - - - - - - - - - - - - - - - - - - - - - - -

**His earliest crimes started at the young age of 18 when he was convicted of theft. Between 1988 and 2000, he was convicted of various crimes including robbery, child sex abuse, illegal sale of pornography, identity theft and forgery.**

When convicted of child rape in 2000, Yoo Young-Chul was imprisoned for more than three years, during which time his wife divorced him and left him as a single man upon his release.

Directly following his release from prison (on 11<sup>th</sup> September 2003), the twisted ex-convict set about maiming and tearing flesh by means of disembowelling and clubbing stray canines to death. This was Young-Chul's way of practising what he had devised for his future criminal activities. The killer carried a knife and constructed his very own homemade hammer, because they were lightweight, easy-to-conceal weapons. It was only after he felt that he had enough practice at slaughtering dogs that he then moved onto his final series of killings.

It was a mere fortnight after his release from his previous prison sentence that Yoo Young-Chul targeted a rich elderly couple in the district of Gangnam Gu, Seoul, where he broke into their home and stabbed the elderly male in the throat. While his screaming wife attended his injury, Yoo Young-Chul proceeded to smash both victims in the back of their skulls with his homemade hammer.

After a few days of killing wealthy and helpless elderly victims, he then moved on to murdering prostitutes after one of his girlfriends found out about his murderous crimes and left him. In Spring 2004, the killer lured a working girl back to his apartment where he then beat her to death with his hammer, decapitated her, smashed her head into an unrecognisable state, mutilated her body and then disposed of the corpse in a nearby construction site. This became his modus operandi for nine further victims.

After murdering eight adults and a baby during his killing spree of wealthy victims, and 11 prostitutes, Yoo Young-Chul was finally arrested on 15<sup>th</sup> July 2004. When on trial, he admitted to killing 21 people in total although one case was dropped due to a technicality.

On 19<sup>th</sup> June 2005, the killer was sentenced to death by the Supreme Court, which proved controversial within the judicial system. Although legal, the death penalty had not been issued for eight years prior to the sentencing. Yoo Young-Chul is currently on death row, awaiting execution by hanging.

*ABOVE: Yoo Young-Chul (top-centre, yellow rain coat) watches as police investigators search for the remains of his victims buried in Seoul*

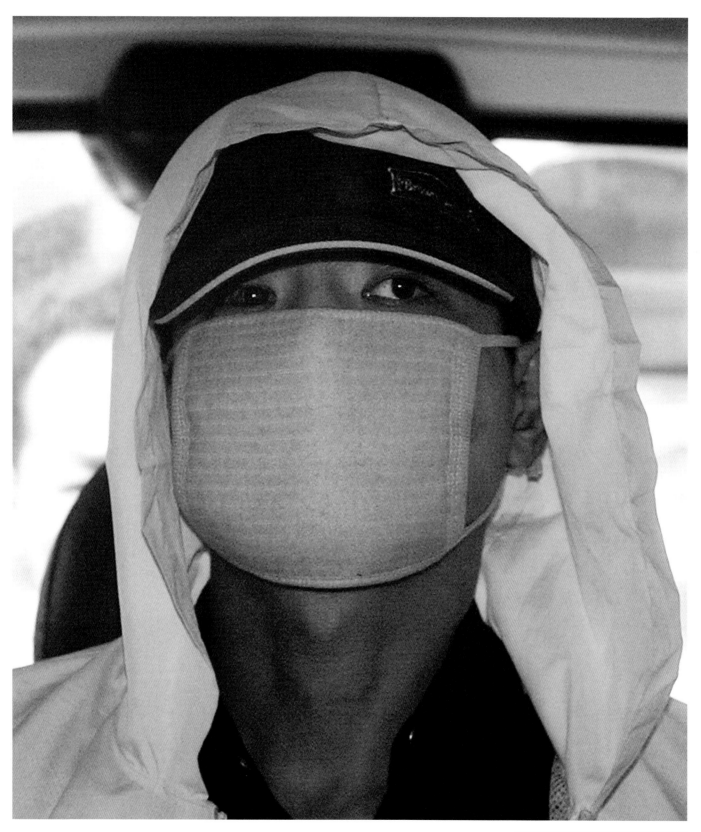

*ABOVE: Yoo Young-Chul being escorted by South Korean
police to a suspected murder site in July 2004*

# Derrick Todd Lee

Derrick Todd Lee, a Louisiana native, was in trouble with the law from a young age. At 16 years old, he was caught peeping into women's homes and more offences followed.

---

**Burglary, assault, trespassing and stalking became routine for Lee, yet his worst offences would be those that saw him placed on death row – for the rape and murder of seven women that earned him the nickname the "Baton Rouge Serial Killer".**

Lee never held a steady job, occasionally working in construction or driving a lorry. Outwardly, he seemed easy-going, able to quickly charm women, and would often quote from the Bible. This "nice guy" façade hid his true nature. While Lee is suspected of being involved in murders from as early as 1991, it was the murders he committed in the early years of the new millennium that saw him dubbed the "Baton Rouge Serial Killer".

In 2002, Charlotte Pace, a graduate student at Louisiana State University, was sexually molested and stabbed to death. DNA evidence linked Pace's murder to one eight months prior. Nurse Gina Green, who also lived near the Louisiana State campus, was sexually molested and strangled to death. Besides the DNA, the only other similarity was that both women's cell phones were stolen. When the nude body of Pat Kinamore was discovered sexually assaulted and stabbed in the neck, the killer was gaining in confidence.

Baton Rouge police now knew they were hunting a serial killer, but there would be more victims before he was caught. The body of Treneisha Dene Colomb, a marine, was discovered in woods three days after she disappeared. She, too, had been sexually assaulted then bludgeoned to death. Feeling the public pressure, the police joined forces with the FBI to create a profile of the killer, yet progress in the investigation continued to lag. Although Lee is African American, the killer was believed to be a white man based on old eyewitness accounts. This gave Lee the chance to strike again. In March 2003, the body of Louisiana State doctoral student Carrie Yoder was discovered in water near to where Pat had been found – she had been beaten and strangled to death.

A new task force was created to catch the killer, but still Lee had the chance to murder Lillian Robinson and dump her body in the same place as two other victims. Another woman, Melinda McGhee, also disappeared during this time. Her body was never discovered.

Success made Lee bold, but he couldn't escape the DNA evidence. When a new composite sketch closely resembled Lee, he was brought in for a DNA sample. He provided one, then immediately fled the state. With the help of the FBI, Lee was arrested in Atlanta, Georgia, in May 2003. Psychiatric evaluations determined that Lee had an IQ of just 65 but it was decided he was capable of standing trial and he was connected to the seven murders. He was convicted of two and sentenced to die by lethal injection; a sentence which was never carried out. Lee died on 21st January 2016, at The Lane Memorial Hospital, Zachary, Louisiana, from heart disease.

*ABOVE: A wanted flier depicts serial murder suspect Derrick Todd Lee at Georgia Bureau of Investigation headquarters in May 2003*

*OPPOSITE: Derrick Todd Lee appears in Fulton County Superior Court for an extradition hearing on 28th May 2003 in Atlanta, Georgia*

# Anthony Hardy

Anthony John Hardy, the son of a coal miner, was born in Burton-upon-Trent, Staffordshire, in 1951 but would gain notoriety as "The Camden Ripper".

**At school, Hardy was a diligent, driven pupil who used his education to escape the lower middle-class lifestyle of his childhood. Having gained a degree in engineering, Hardy became the manager of a successful engineering company.**

Hardy married and moved to Tasmania with his wife but, in 1982, he bludgeoned his wife with a frozen bottle of water then tried to drown her. The charges were dropped but his wife divorced him in 1986. After the divorce, Hardy was diagnosed as having bipolar disorder.

His deteriorating mental and physical health brought about mood swings and drunken, violent behaviour and theft. In 1998, Hardy was arrested on suspicion of raping a prostitute. Owing to a lack of evidence, the charge was eventually dropped.

In 2000, the Metropolitan police attended a report of vandalism at a block of council flats in Camden, north London. Hardy was back in the UK and a neighbour suspected him of damaging her door. Acting on the concerns of other neighbours, officers entered and searched Hardy's flat. In the locked bedroom, they discovered the naked corpse of a prostitute called Sally White. Flawed forensic evidence provided by Dr Freddy Patel indicated that Sally had died from a heart attack, and not foul play. Consequently, Hardy spent a spell in prison for the vandalism alone.

The Sally White case was reopened in 2002 after a homeless man found bin bags containing the dismembered remains of two women in wheelie bins near Hardy's flat. The killer, aware of the renewed police interest in him, changed his appearance and went on the run. He was identified and arrested at Great Ormond Street Hospital in London on 2nd January 2003.

A police search of Hardy's flat provided damning forensic evidence that two women had been murdered and butchered there. A bloodied hacksaw was discovered while an electric jigsaw was removed for forensic examination. Officers observed pornographic magazines scattered around the flat. Blood was found in the bathroom and a devil's mask had been placed alongside a "Sally White RIP" note while a woman's torso was found wrapped in bin liners.

Faced with this overwhelming evidence, Hardy met every police question with "no comment". He was charged with the brutal murders of three women – including Sally White – and, at his trial in November 2003, Hardy changed his plea to "guilty" on all three counts of murder. He was convicted and sentenced to life in prison.

Detectives believe Hardy committed at least two more prostitute murders in London and suspect his involvement in up to six unsolved murder cases sharing similarities with his Camden killings. However, a lack of evidence has prevented officers from adding these crimes to Hardy's charge sheet.

Dr Freddy Patel – the forensic pathologist who had concluded that Hardy's first known victim, Sally White, had died from natural causes – was later suspended from the official register of forensic pathologists. In 2012, Patel was "struck off" the General Medical Council's register.

*LEFT: A court artist sketches a portrait of murder suspect Anthony Hardy following his court appearance*

*OPPOSITE: A police diver emerges from the water with what police describe as a gun during a search for evidence of Hardy's victims in the Regents Canal, London*

# Robert Pickton

Robert William "Willie" Pickton, a third generation pig farmer, was born in 1949 in British Columbia, Canada. Along with his brother, he inherited and operated the family pig farm at Port Coquitlam.

In 1997, Pickton was accused of the attempted murder of a prostitute. The case was dropped because prosecutors believed the drug-addled victim would be unable to provide a reliable account of the alleged attack – even though both she and Pickton had received hospital treatment for stab wounds, and the key to a pair of handcuffs hanging from the prostitute's wrist had been found in Pickton's pocket.

Pickton had a long association with the prostitutes of Vancouver. The Picktons had converted a building on their farm into an infamous party venue called "The Piggy Palace". This building became the setting for wild, drunken raves at which guests would be "entertained" by prostitutes. The Pickton's pig farm was patrolled by a vicious 600-pound boar, which was "better than any guard dog" and savaged any intruders – and any victims trying to escape.

In 1999, police officers received a tip-off that Pickton kept human flesh in freezers on his farm. A search warrant was issued but no search was carried out. In 2002, another warrant was issued for the farm, for unlicensed firearms. The search recovered items belonging to a missing woman.

Officers from the Royal Canadian Mounted Police searched the farm again and found human remains, skulls cut in half and filled with feet and hands, a jawbone and teeth, clothing drenched in blood, and DNA from 33 women. They also recovered a pistol with a dildo attached as a rudimentary silencer. This dildo was found to retain DNA from Pickton and one of his victims. Also recovered were two pairs of faux fur-lined handcuffs and a set of night vision goggles.

Pickton was arrested and, while in custody, boasted to a fellow detainee [an undercover police officer] that he had tortured and killed 49 women, but had wanted to round the count up to an even 50.

Police and forensic anthropologists continued their painstaking, soil-sieving investigations at the pig farm. But there wasn't much evidence; it had been eaten. Pickton would lure Vancouver prostitutes to his farm for sex. During sex, he would become violent, accuse them of theft and become enraged. He would handcuff them, shoot or strangle them, then bleed, gut and dismember their corpses. Pickton disposed of the body parts in two ways. First he fed the remains to his pigs. Second he ground the human flesh into mince, mixed it with pork, then sold it in packs to meat processing businesses in the Fraser Valley, and to his friends and family.

Pickton's trial was long and legally confused. In 2007, the jury found him not guilty on six counts of first-degree murder, but guilty on six counts of second-degree murder. On 11th December, Pickton was sentenced to life imprisonment with no possibility of parole for 25 years.

*ABOVE LEFT: Robert Pickton is shown in this undated image from a television screen. Pickton and his brother operated a drinking club frequented by bikers and prostitutes near their pig farm outside Vancouver, Canada*

*OPPOSITE: Royal Canadian Mounted Police investigators work with a drilling crew and heavy machinery during an investigation at the Picktons's pig farm*

# Levi Bellfield

Born in May 1968 in Middlesex, Levi Bellfield was brought up in southwest London. His first conviction, for burglary, came in 1981 and was followed by further convictions for theft and driving offences.

**The father of 11 children is a former bouncer and wheel clamper, described by police as a violent, cunning man. Bellfield's ex-partners described him as charming and lovely, before he turned nasty and violent. He scoured the streets of London and surrounding areas that he knew intimately, looking for unsuspecting victims.**

On 21st March 2002, 13-year-old Milly Dowler went missing from Walton-on-Thames. Although police didn't know it at the time, Bellfield was the man responsible for the attempted abduction of 12-year-old Rachel Cowles, just one day before Milly's disappearance. In September that year, Milly's body was found in Hampshire. In the early hours of 4th February 2003, Bellfield had already struck. This time, his victim was 19-year-old Marsha McDonnell who was hit by a hammer over the head as she made the short walk from the bus stop to her home in Hampton. Marsha was the first murder victim of an attacker targeting vulnerable women at or around bus stops in southwest London. The attacks were ongoing between 2001 and 2004. In May 2004, Kate Sheedy (18) was purposely run over by Bellfield in Isleworth yet, despite suffering multiple injuries, survived the horrendous attack. French student Amelie Delagrange (22) was found with serious head injuries on 19th August 2004 at Twickenham Green. She later died in hospital and police were confident that Amelie was attacked by the same man who killed Marsha.

Bellfield was found guilty of the murders of Marsha McDonnell and Amelie Delagrange and the attempted murder of Kate Sheedy in February 2008 and sentenced to life imprisonment. Just over two years later in March 2010, he was charged with the kidnap and murder of Milly Dowler. He was found guilty in June 2011.

Police believe that Bellfield's crimes go back much further than the beginning of the 21st century and may even stretch back to 1980 when the murderer was just 12 years old. A girl attending the same school as Bellfield was found murdered and her killer has never been caught. Many crimes from the 1990s are also thought to have been carried out by Bellfield, including the abduction and murder of 25-year-old Melanie Hall in 1996, who disappeared outside a nightclub in Bath. More than 13 years later, Melanie's body was discovered in a bin bag on a slip road of the M5 near Thornbury in Gloucestershire. The young woman had been beaten with a blunt instrument over the head, which had fractured her skull, cheek and jaw before she died. Bellfield was known to have driven a Ford around the time Melanie was abducted, and keys for this make of car were found close to her body while Bellfield was known to travel regularly to Bristol, close to Bath, to score drugs.

*ABOVE: Levi Bellfield was found guilty of two murders and one attempted murder in February 2008*

# Leonard Fraser

Leonard Fraser became a serial rapist and serial killer, convicted of the brutal killing of nine-year-old Keyra Steinhardt, in Rockhampton in 1999. Prior to this, he had already served 20 years in prison for raping a number of women.

**Fraser's childhood was outwardly normal, but he struggled in school. Although he dreamed of joining the Hell's Angels motorcycle gang and dabbled in crime as a teenager, there was nothing to suggest that Fraser the car thief, pimp and robber would evolve to become a brutal rapist and merciless killer.**

When Leonard John Fraser – born in Ingham, Queensland, Australia – was convicted in 1972 of committing a series of robberies and sentenced to serve five years hard labour, police officers investigating his offences were unaware that, two months before, he had raped a French tourist in Sydney's Botanical Gardens.

Fraser was tried and convicted of two rapes and two attempted rapes in 1974. During the trial, the court-appointed psychiatrist observed that the rapist was beyond help – he was so dangerous because he had no conscience, and actually believed that his victims really wanted to have sex with him.

Fraser eventually confessed to five murders. Women victims had either been flogged to death, or bled to death like slaughtered animals. At his subsequent trial for the ferocious killings, he was described by the judge as a sexual predator who was a danger to both the community and his fellow prisoners. Inmates who shared the Wolston Correction Centre with Fraser had an apt name for their violent, unpredictable, serial killing cellmate – they called him "Lenny the Loon".

Fraser was a "souvenir" keeper and hoarded many items taken from his victims, including three ponytails cut from the heads of three victims. However, the owners of these ponytails were not amongst Fraser's known victims and these women have never been identified.

Fraser had a signature, "calling card" method of seizing his victims. He would follow women as they walked along quiet stretches of road. He would sneak up behind them, grab an arm, twist it, and force it up behind his victim's back. Having gained total control of the woman, he would propel her to a secluded place, and subject her to a violent rape and hideous death.

Fraser was alleged to have murdered a 14-year-old called Natasha Ryan. However, Ryan made a sensational reappearance during Fraser's trial, five years after she had been placed on the police missing person's list. It was then revealed that she had been living in secret with her boyfriend. When Ryan returned from the dead, she tried to sell her story to the press for an estimated $250,000.

At Fraser's trial on 13th June 2003, the judge described him as an "untreatable psychopath" before convicting him on two counts of murder, and one count of manslaughter, and sentencing him to serve three indefinite jail terms. On 31st December 2006, Fraser died in his sleep in hospital, from a fatal heart attack. Criminologists suspect he took the secrets of many unsolved murders to the grave.

*ABOVE: Leonard Fraser is escorted from Police HQ in August 2001*

# William Lee "Cody" Neal

There was nothing on the surface of William Lee Neal's typical American childhood to indicate the killer he would become.

**His father was a hard-working air force officer and his mother a loving, soft-spoken woman. His parents never argued and always told Neal to do what was right. Growing up, he wanted to be an FBI agent or a minister, but there was trouble beneath the surface.**

His sisters would purposely hurt themselves then blame Neal, whose father would then beat him with a belt. When his father drank, he would drag Neal to bars and purposely embarrass his son in front of the other drunks. As a teenager, Neal was seduced by an older, married woman who he believed passed some sort of darkness onto him. Soon after their relationship ended, he molested a younger girl.

Neal became a serial womaniser and molester, claiming to have had thousands of sexual conquests. Nicknaming himself "Cody" and "Wild Bill Cody", Neal was highly manipulative, able to convince women of whatever they wanted to hear. He was also jealous, obsessive and paranoid. He married four times and though his wives suffered his sadistic abuse, they would survive his rage. Later girlfriends would not be so lucky.

One week in 1998, Neal snapped. He had been living in Colorado with his girlfriend, Rebecca Holberton, for two years and, during that time, borrowed over $70,000 from her. At the same time, he had a secret second girlfriend, Candace Walters. He owed her an additional $6,000. In June, Neal discovered that Holberton wanted to kick him out of the house as soon as she got her money back and also that Walters was threatening to reveal their relationship to Holberton if her loan was not repaid. Instead of coming clean, Neal went to the store and bought eyebolts, nylon rope, duct tape and a seven-and-a-half pound splitting maul – half axe, half sledgehammer.

After convincing Holberton that he had a surprise for her – implying it was her money – he covered her head with a blanket and bashed her skull in with the splitting maul. Then he wrapped her body in plastic and leaned it up against the wall. Three days later, he took Walters to the house, sat her in the same place as Holberton, then killed her with four strokes of the axe. Neal was not done yet.

Three days after Walters's murder, he brought acquaintance Suzanne Scott to the house and tied her to a mattress, leaving her there as he fetched his third girlfriend, Angela Fite. After showing Fite the women's bodies and telling her: "Welcome to my mortuary," he forced Scott to watch as he murdered Fite. Afterwards, he sodomised and raped Scott at gunpoint. All night, he sat with her, talking and holding her hand. The next morning, he returned Scott to her apartment and she called the police.

Neal was convicted of murder in 1999 and placed on death row but, in 2003, his sentence was commuted to life in prison.

*LEFT: In the wrong hands, a splitting maul – as used by William Lee Neal – can be a very destructive weapon*

# Cedric Maake

Known as the "Wemmer Pan Killer", Cedric Maake was responsible for at least 27 murders committed between 1996 and 1997.

**What makes his heinous crimes even more chilling is the fact that Maake did not stick to one modus operandi. Unlike other serial killers, South African Maake used five different ways to butcher his victims.**

Wemmer Pan, the area of Johannesburg where most of Maake's victims were targeted, did not at first offer police murder scenes that provided a link. The South African Police Service (SAPS) actually thought to begin with that they had two serial killers on the loose because of the methods used and two different criminal profiles were compiled.

The first was for the Wemmer Pan murderer who had two distinct patterns of killing. Both lone men and women were targeted and bludgeoned to death with rocks. In addition, a second group of victims involved couples whom Maake – born in 1965 – attacked as they sat in their cars. The men were shot and the women raped. In the second profile, the murderer was dubbed the "Hammer murderer" for inner city attacks on tailors, killed in their shops by blows from a hammer.

Geographic profiling later showed that Maake's victims were all killed around two specific residences – that of his brother and the home of his girlfriend. In fact, Geographic Information Systems (GIS) and crime mapping technology provided the geographical extent of the serial killer's target sites and was eventually one of the earliest uses of the system that helped in a successful prosecution. Maake slipped up when he left a ticket at one of the shops where he carried out a brutal hammer attack, which also helped link him to both profiles – his signature on the ticket placed him at the scene of the crime.

He was arrested in December 1997 when police were able to connect him to the Wemmer Pan murders. Maake co-operated with police and confessed to 35 counts of murder, 28 attempted murders, the rape of 15 women, 46 counts of aggravated robbery and the unlawful possession of firearms and ammunition. One month after his arrest, he also confessed to the "hammer" murders but, in court, he pleaded "not guilty" to all charges. Following a lengthy investigation and subsequent trial, Maake was convicted in September 2000 of 27 murders, 26 attempted murders, 14 counts of rape, 41 aggravated robberies and countless less serious offences. He was found guilty of 114 crimes in total and was sentenced to 1,340 years imprisonment including 27 life sentences for the murders.

It had taken Brigadier Piet Byleveld six months to catch Maake, a fresh-faced 32-year-old, but he knew he had his man as soon as he took the suspect into custody. Piet got to know Maake and discovered that he was close to his wife, but closer still to his mother. He knew Maake hated his father with a vengeance. The first thing Piet organised was a blood sample for DNA analysis. Forensics worked around the clock and came up with a match. Maake was the serial killer. Once he was caught and "nailed" by the DNA evidence, Maake literally threw his own faeces around his cell and at the two guards watching him in Brixton Prison, Johannesburg. It took Piet three hours to calm the serial killer down and over the next few days, accompanied by police officers, Maake went to the murder scenes where he described his crimes and spoke of the items or "trophies" he had taken from his victims including clothing and shoes. These were later found, at his mother's house near Tzaneen, while during the same trip Maake showed Piet where to find the pistol he had used in the shootings.

*ABOVE: Cedric Maake was unusual for a serial killer in that he targeted different types of victims in different areas of Johannesburg*

# Joseph Edward Duncan III

Joseph Edward Duncan III was just 15 years old when his criminal career began in 1978 and he sexually assaulted a boy in his hometown of Tacoma, Washington, in the United States.

- - - - - - - - - - - - - - - - - - - - - - - - - - - - - - - - - - - - - - - - - - - - -

**In 1980, he was sentenced to 20 years in prison for the rape of the nine-year-old. He told his psychiatrist upon his incarceration that he estimated he had raped 13 younger boys by the time he was 16 (it had taken the authorities a year to catch him). He was released on parole in 1994, but sent back to prison three years later for violating his parole.**

When eventually released, Duncan reverted to his former ways. Brenda Groene, her partner and her 13-year-old son were found dead at their home in Kootenai County, Idaho in May 2005. The victim's two other children were missing.

Nearly two months later, police found Shasta Groene, eight, with Duncan, but Dylan, nine, was found dead near St Regis, Montana. Duncan was arrested for Shasta's kidnap and charged with the murder of four members of the young girl's family.

It was at this point that police linked Duncan to the murder of two girls in Seattle aged 11 and 9 (between 1994 and 1997) and 10-year-old Anthony Martinez in California, whom he forced at knifepoint into his vehicle when the small boy refused to help Duncan look for a "lost" cat.

He received six life sentences for the kidnap and murders of Shasta's mother, brother and her mother's partner. Duncan was also convicted of kidnapping the little girl and her brother Dylan, and for murdering the young boy for which he received three death sentences and three life sentences. In addition, he received two life sentences for the murder of Anthony Martinez, although he was not convicted of the girls's murders.

Duncan, a serial killer who has spent most of his adult life in prison, now sits on death row in a federal prison.

*RIGHT: Joseph Edward Duncan during a plea agreement and sentencing hearing in the court room of the Kootenai County Jail in October 2006*

ABOVE: A huge billboard along State Highway 95 north of Coeur d' Alene, Idaho with the photos of Shasta Groene and Dylan Groene in July 2005

BELOW: Steve Groene holds up a message from family members after Joseph Edward Duncan entered into a plea agreement

# Todd Kohlhepp

Realtor and pilot turned serial killer, Todd Kohlhepp, now faces a lifetime in jail for multiple charges including kidnapping and murdering seven victims.

**Kohlhepp's killings were carried out over a shocking 13-year period. To date, the killer has pleaded guilty to seven crimes.**

Todd Kohlhepp was born in Florida on 7th March 1971. He was raised in South Carolina and Georgia with his mother and stepfather. He had a troubled childhood and psychological reports revealed that Kohlhepp had an unhealthy relationship with his stepfather. From a young age, he displayed behavioural problems often recognised in troubled children. He was described as having an "explosive" temper and, as a young boy, he rarely interacted with other children. In addition to this, he would carry out violent acts towards animals, which included shooting a dog with a BB gun and poisoning a fish with Clorox. Due to his inability to engage with children of his age, Kohlhepp was admitted to a mental hospital in Georgia and spent almost four months in the establishment as an inpatient.

In 1986, Kohlhepp moved to Arizona to live with his biological father following his mother and stepfather's break-up. It was during this period that he committed his first crime in Tempe. Kohlhepp kidnapped a fourteen-year-old girl, tied her up, taped her mouth shut and raped her. Following the attack, he walked the victim home and threatened to kill her siblings if she told anyone about the assault. Kohlhepp was later charged with kidnapping, sexual assault and committing a crime against a child. This was the first of many violent crimes Kohlhepp would commit during the course of his life as a free man. The perpetrator was just fifteen at the time of his first assault.

In 1987, Kohlhepp pleaded guilty to the kidnapping charge, and the additional charges against him were dropped. The verdict: he was sentenced to 15 years in jail and was registered as a sex offender. Interestingly, the judge in the case commented on his academic abilities stating he was "very bright and should be advanced academically," yet she informed those in court that he was "behaviourally and emotionally dangerous".

During his imprisonment, Kohlhepp enrolled as a student and completed a bachelor's degree in computer science at Central Arizona College. In August 2001, soon after his release from prison, he relocated to South Carolina to be closer to his mother. A company in Spartanburg employed Kohlhepp as a graphic designer; he worked there for two years. He then completed his second degree at the University of South Carolina, where he studied business administration marketing. Despite his mental fragility and violent tendencies, Kohlhepp excelled in academia and showed a great deal of potential.

On 6th November 2003, just two years after Kohlhepp's release, four people were found dead inside Superbike Motorsports, a popular motorbike shop in Chesnee, South Carolina. They had been shot multiple times. The victims of the homicide were identified as owner Scott Ponder (30); Brian Lucas (30); Chris Sherbert (26) and Beverly Guy (52), who was Ponder's mother. The perpetrator behind the quadruple murder would remain a mystery for over a decade. Kohlhepp didn't confess to the crime until November 2016 and, by this point, he had killed again.

On 30th June 2006, Kohlhepp managed to obtain a real estate license despite his criminal record. It was later discovered that he had lied about a felony charge on his application. He started to build a firm that would eventually employ a dozen agents; Kohlhepp quickly became one of the most successful working agents in his region. It was during this period that he committed a multitude of violent, disturbing crimes.

Kohlhepp was eventually arrested in November 2016, aged 45, when Spartanburg county sheriff's deputies found Kala Brown (30), who had been incarcerated in a metal storage container, and the body of Charlie Carver, her boyfriend, on his property. The police had tracked Brown down, after tracing the couple's last-recorded mobile signals. Kala Brown and her boyfriend had been missing since August. Brown later told investigators that she witnessed Kohlhepp shoot and kill her boyfriend whose body was discovered in a shallow grave. Kohlhepp later revealed that he kept Brown alive because she hadn't done anything wrong and he didn't want to hurt her. While Brown was held in captivity, she was fed once a day.

Soon after his arrest in November 2016, two additional bodies were found on Kohlhepp's 100-acre property. They were identified as Johnny Joe Coxie (29), and his wife, Meagan Leigh McCraw Coxie (26) from Spartanburg. The pair had been reported missing on 22nd December 2015, and were originally hired by Kohlhepp to work on his property. The perpetrator shot Meagan Coxie in the head on 25th or 26th December after holding her against her will. He reportedly killed Johnny Coxie a week earlier. A post-mortem examination found he was killed by a gunshot wound to the torso. Both bodies had been buried recklessly in shallow graves and fully clothed. They were identified through their extensive tattoos and dental records.

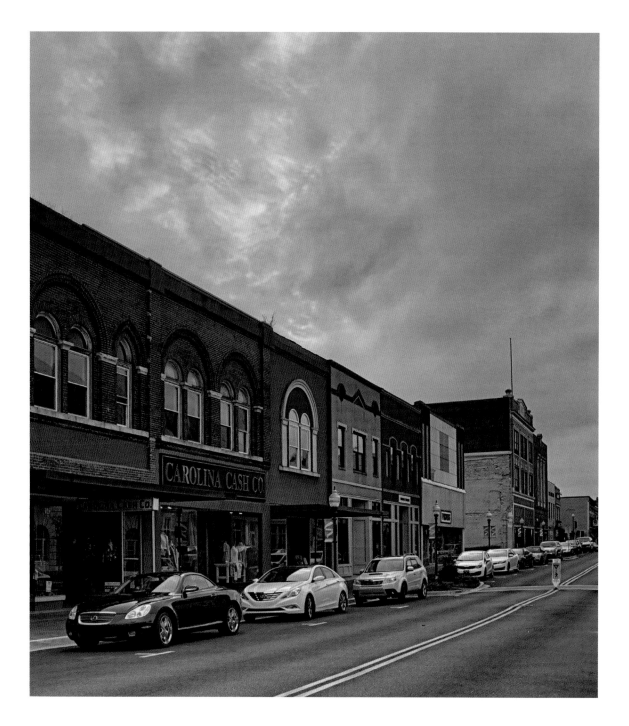

*ABOVE: A street in Spartanburg, South Carolina, where Kohlhepp was employed as a graphic designer for two years*

Kohlhepp was later charged with murder for the deaths of Carver and the Coxies. In addition to this, he was charged with multiple kidnapping and weapon charges connected to the homicides.

His current status of 'held without bond' remains fixed and demonstrates the severity of the crime. Kohlhepp was charged with four counts of murder in relation to the Chesnee shootings and one further count for kidnapping, in relation to Brown's abduction and holding her against her will. Kohlhepp was last scheduled to appear in court in January 2017. However, the killer's attorney waived their right to appearance.

# Dr Harold Shipman

One of the most prolific serial killers in history, Dr Harold Shipman murdered more than 250 people between 1975 and 2000, all of them trusting patients of the Greater Manchester GP.

**Though his victims, both men and women, ranged from 41 to 93 years old, the majority were older women whom he killed by administering lethal doses of diamorphine. It's possible his obsession was spawned by witnessing his mother's death from terminal lung cancer.**

At only 17, Shipman watched doctors visit their home to administer morphine and ease her pain. However, others believe he simply enjoyed the feeling of controlling life and death as Shipman was no angel of mercy. The majority of his patients were not even ill.

Shipman was in practice for over 24 years, visiting his patients at home and murdering them with deadly doses of morphine or insulin. It was a local undertaker, Alan Massey, who first began to suspect something was wrong when he noticed that Dr Shipman's patients

died at a higher rate than other doctors. Also, upon arriving to collect the bodies, Massey never saw anything in the house to indicate the deceased had been ill. Shipman, with his reassuring bedside manner, convinced Massey nothing sinister was going on, but Massey's daughter, Debbie, was not so easily swayed.

Debbie spoke to Dr Susan Booth, who had countersigned many of Shipman's requests for cremation and who also found his behaviour suspicious. The women's concerns finally landed in the hands of the police but, after reviewing Shipman's records, they felt nothing was amiss. They did not realise Shipman was a master forger who had doctored his reports to match his victims's causes of death and the doctor was left free to kill again.

It was Angela Woodruff, a solicitor and daughter of Shipman's last victim, who finally exposed the doctor. Her mother, Kathleen Grundy, was a healthy, incredibly active and wealthy ex-mayor. After friends discovered her dead at home, fully clothed and sitting in her chair, they rang Shipman who said that an autopsy need not be performed as he had seen her just a few hours earlier. When solicitors contacted Woodruff stating they had a copy of her mother's will, she was immediately suspicious. She had handled all her mother's affairs. The will, which left hundreds of thousands of pounds to Shipman, was a badly typed, poorly forged fake.

This time, the police believed the suspicions and exhumed Grundy's body. Hers was the first of many to be examined and discovered to contain lethal medication which was never prescribed. When the police arrived at Shipman's home with a warrant, he was arrogant and controlling during the interviews.

He denied all charges against him, even after he was convicted of 15 murders and sentenced to life in prison. The Shipman Inquiry, a two-year investigation into his other possible murders, then followed. Beginning in September 2000, it investigated every death ever certified by Shipman.

Meanwhile, the heartless doctor committed suicide in January 2004, hanging himself in his cell at HM Prison Wakefield in West Yorkshire.

*LEFT: Dr Harold Shipman*

# Alexander Spesivtsev

Alexander Nikolayevich Spesivtsev was born in Kemerovo Oblast, Siberia, in 1970. His father abused and tortured his wife and children alike.

----

**In 1991, Spesivtsev murdered his 19-year-old girlfriend in the apartment he shared with his mother, Ludmilla. For this murder Spesivtsev was declared insane and incarcerated in a psychiatric hospital for three years. Upon his release, he returned home to live with Ludmilla – and a ferocious Doberman dog.**

In 1996, Spesivtsev's neighbour, already incensed by horrible smells and loud rock music emanating from his flat, noticed a water leak. No one answered the plumber's knock, so he forced open the front door – and called the police. In the confusion, Spesivtsev escaped.

The walls of Spesivtsev's apartment were drenched with blood. In the kitchen, officers discovered bowls filled with pieces of human bodies. In the living room, they observed a human ribcage, while, in the bathroom, the bath was found to contain a mutilated, headless corpse. On the sofa, sat a girl barely alive, with multiple stab wounds to her stomach and chest. The officers rushed 15-year-old Olga to hospital, where she was able to provide a horrific account of what had happened to her. Seventeen hours later, Olga died from her terrible injuries.

Olga and two 13-year-old girl friends had helped Spesivtsev's mother, Ludmilla, carry bags of groceries up to her apartment. Ludmilla enticed the girls into the flat, where they were trapped by Spesivtsev's ferocious dog. Spesivtsev then beat and raped them, before killing one of the younger girls. He then forced the two surviving girls to butcher their friend in the bath. Ludmilla took the resulting "meat" and made it into soup, which Olga was forced to eat before Spesivtsev set his dog on the second 13-year-old girl, who was ripped apart.

Police found 80 items of blood stained clothing, 40 pieces of jewellery taken from victims, photographs of victims and a diary kept by Spesivtsev in which he detailed the murders of 19 girls.

Spesivtsev was later arrested following the rape of another woman. He then confessed to killing the 19 girls identified in his diary.

At Spesivtsev's trial, it emerged that he had developed a murderous loathing for the local street children, and regarded himself as a crusader trying to clean up the streets of his town. His mother had helped him lure children to their apartment, cooked "meat" cut from the victim's corpses, and then disposed of the body parts by dropping them into the River Aba in the dead of night. Her grandmotherly "babushka" appearance enabled her to pass unnoticed as she carried the grizzly evidence to the river.

Believed to have killed as many as 80 street children, Spesivtsev – who earned multiple nicknames such as "Sasha", "The Novokuznetsk Monster", "The Cannibal of Siberia" and "The Siberian Ripper" – was convicted of multiple counts of murder and committed to a secure mental hospital in 1999. At a subsequent trial, Ludmilla Spesivtsev was convicted of aiding her cannibalistic son and received a life prison sentence.

*ABOVE: A Doberman Pinscher, Alexander Spesivtsev's weapon of choice*

# Moses Sithole

Moses Sithole was born in 1964 in an impoverished part of the Transvaal Province of South Africa.

---

**When Sithole was five, his father died and his mother, unable to support her family financially, abandoned her children. Sithole and his four brothers and sisters were sent to live in an orphanage in Kwazulu Natal. The children were subjected to cruel, systematic abuse and Sithole tried to escape three times. Eventually, he went to live with his older brother Patrick.**

In 1987, Sithole began a six-year sentence for rape in Boksburg prison. While a prisoner, Sithole was himself anally and orally raped by fellow inmates. Once released from jail in 1994, Sithole initiated his own brutal campaign of rape and murder.

A charming and handsome man, Sithole posed as a successful businessman with jobs to offer to women as employees in his bogus charity. Young women, eager for work, proved to be easy prey. Sithole charmed them and gained their trust and would accompany them in broad daylight to his isolated "business headquarters". Once they were out of sight and hearing and completely isolated, Sithole overpowered his victims, tied them up, raped them and strangled them with their own underwear.

This simple method proved fatally efficient – by 1995, he had raped and murdered 30 women and evaded all attempts to apprehend him. Sithole's confidence grew and he took delight in telephoning the families of some of his victims and taunting them.

A task force was set up to probe the case, and confirm common factors. The murderer was improving his technique to maximise the pain inflicted on his victims and increase his pleasure at each kill. He was now using a stick to wind their tights as a garotte round their necks. The progression of his sadistic methods was both shocking and disturbing.

In 1995, a mass grave of Sithole's victims was discovered at the Van Dyk Mine near Boksburg. Forensic experts recovered 10 decomposing corpses from the site, where all the victims were linked to Sithole's fake job offers – he had used his real name when he set up the job interviews and the net was closing.

With his name known, and Sithole still at large, the police released his details to the press to flush him out. The ruthless killer contacted a journalist at the "Star" newspaper, but evaded police attempts to capture him at arranged meeting places. Sithole contacted his brother-in-law, seeking a gun, who informed the police of his request. They set a trap and shot Sithole in the leg and stomach as he charged at them brandishing an axe. Sithole was arrested and taken for surgery at the Pretoria Military Hospital.

Once in custody, Sithole confessed to all the murders. In 1997, Justice David Carstairs, taking into account 38 murders, 40 rapes and six robberies, sentenced Sithole to serve 2,410 years in the maximum security section of Pretoria Central Prison; to serve 930 years before being eligible for parole.

*LEFT: Moses Sithole was shot and wounded when he attacked arresting policemen with an axe in October 1995*

*ABOVE: Members of the South African police force search a Boksburg field where the bodies of ten murdered women victims were found*

Upon arrival at the prison, the convicted killer was diagnosed as HIV positive. Sithole is currently incarcerated in Manguang Correctional centre, Bloemfontein, South Africa.

# Orville Lynn Majors

Orville Lynn Majors was a licensed nurse described by many of his earlier patients as caring, tender and compassionate.

------------------------------------------------------------

**He was a favourite amongst hospital residents and many relatives of his patients would often write to the hospital, commending his work.**

At the end of his medical career, Majors – born on 24th April 1961 in Clinton, Indiana – was working for Vermillion County Hospital, treating his patients as usual, when it was noticed that the hospital death toll had rapidly increased. Over a two-year period (1993–95), the toll rose in excess of 75% annually, leading to an urgent investigation into the deaths.

Despite his seemingly caring manner in front of his patients, it was his attitude and general demeanour behind closed doors that raised concerns amongst other hospital employees. A supervisory study highlighted the fact that the patient death rate almost doubled while Majors was on duty. Alongside further peer reports that he had been administering unauthorised injections to patients, Majors was later fired in 1995. It was at this time that he had his nursing license revoked. Shortly after he lost his job, the death toll at the hospital dropped dramatically.

Due to insufficient evidence, Majors was not arrested until 1997, when his nephew, Jason Crynes, told the police investigators that his uncle had been bragging about killing patients.

During a police search of his property, potassium chloride was found amongst other medical supplies, commonly used for administering injections, in his garage. It was strongly believed that Majors was injecting his elderly patients with the chemical compound as a means of stopping their hearts.

Witness testimony suggested that Majors had always been in the presence of a patient immediately before their death. Just moments before the death of Dorothea Hixon, Majors was seen by the patient's daughter removing a needle from her mother's IV line. He whispered: "It's alright" and proceeded to kiss the patient on the forehead. Within seconds, Dorothea had died. During the trial, one of his colleagues testified that Majors had often disparaged the elderly as "a waste" and referred to his patients and their families as "white trash" and "whiners". This was a total conflict of the reputation for compassion and kindness with which he had long been associated.

Majors was finally convicted of six confirmed murders, however it is believed that he may have committed as many as 130 during a two year period. He was sentenced to a total of 360 years imprisonment, which he is currently serving in Indiana State Prison.

*LEFT: Serial murderer, nurse Orville Lynn Majors standing in front of West General Community Hospital (formerly Vermillion County Hospital) where the murders took place*

# Colin Ireland

Colin Ireland, born on 16th March 1954 in a workhouse in Kent, had an unsettled childhood. He never knew his father, or even who he was, and his extremely young mother struggled to raise him due to severe poverty.

- - - - - - - - - - - - - - - - - - - - - - - - - - - - - - - - - - - - - - - - - - - - - - - - -

**Mother and son moved many times and became residents of a home for homeless women twice during Ireland's childhood years. At one point, he was taken into foster care because of financial struggles, although a number of years were spent living with his maternal grandparents. He was bullied at school and would often play truant to avoid the taunts from other children about his poor background.**

In adulthood, Ireland was no stranger to prison and was convicted of burglary in 1975, and "demanding with menace" in 1977, serving time for each offence. His crimes intensified in 1993 when Ireland murdered five men after he made a New Year's Resolution to become a serial killer. Four of the murders occurred in the space of just 17 days.

He was a meticulous killer who prepared for each murder and thoroughly cleaned the crime scene after he had finished. Prior to the deaths of his victims, he interrogated them for money in order to keep funding his killing spree. Ireland's target victims were homosexual men but, during police interviews, he maintained that he had no vendetta against homosexuals but chose them simply because they were easy targets. He would meet potential victims at The Coleherne, a pub in Fulham, west London that was popular with members of the gay community. It was here that he chose his targets by pretending to be a homosexual, attracted to them, before luring them back to their own flats.

Ireland's modus operandi was to either suffocate or strangle his victims while they were in compromising positions; either bound or handcuffed to a bed. Each victim was tortured having been promised sex games that Ireland had no intention of carrying out. London's gay community was terrorised, while Ireland was simply keen to establish how easy it was to become a serial killer, how to get away with it and whether, once caught, it would make him famous.

There was no known sexual motive behind the attacks, although in all of the cases the victims were found naked. In the case of Andrew Collier, Ireland's fourth victim, he also killed the victim's pet cat and placed the dead animal over the corpse with the cat's mouth over the dead man's penis and its tail in Collier's mouth. Ireland was not as thorough when cleaning up this particular crime scene, and left behind a fingerprint on the window frame.

On 24th June, police issued a description of a man seen with the fifth victim on a train between Charing Cross station and Hither Green. From this information they were able to generate an E-fit, which was

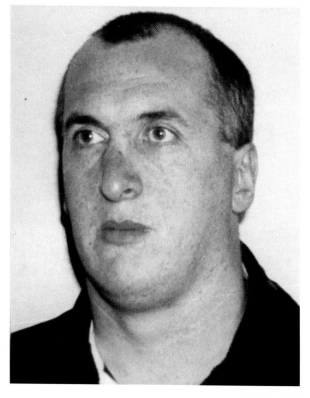

*ABOVE: Colin Ireland*

promptly released asking for the identity of the man and requesting that he contact them. Concerned that he may be recognised, Ireland told his solicitor that he was with the victim on the night he died but wasn't the murderer, and that he left the victim in the company of another man. He told the same story to police, believing that they would just let him go in return for having come forward. However, the fingerprint found at Collier's property was matched to Ireland and, unable to keep up the pretence, he confessed to all five murders.

Ireland pleaded guilty and was sentenced to life imprisonment. He died in Wakefield Prison in 2012.

# Sergei Martynov

The Voronezh Region Court in Russia sentenced multiple killer Sergei (also spelled Sergey) Martynov to life in prison in 2012.

- - - - - - - - - - - - - - - - - - - - - - - - - - - - - - - - - - - - - - - - - - - -

**The homeless murderer was convicted of using a knife, scalpel and other implements to slaughter eight people across a number of regions from Vladimir Region to Yekaterinburg. The reasons given by Martynov for his killing spree, carried out between 2005 and 2010, was his dislike for certain victims and his wish to rid the world of "useless people".**

His final victim, a homeless woman, was strangled with a belt not far from the city of Voronezh, but he was also found guilty of seven other deaths, inflicting severe and grave injuries, "sexual violence" and rape of an eight-year-old girl.

The 50-year-old had already been given a 14-year sentence for the rape and murder of an unknown woman in 1992 but, on his release in 2005, he resumed the killing and the court at his trial heard how his crimes were "notable for their special cynicism", while he "committed outrages upon many of the bodies". In 2005, he attacked a 17-year-old girl, slashing her face with a razor blade, but a court freed him and he simply disappeared for a time. His methods tended to follow the same pattern.

Martynov would generally befriend a homeless woman with a drinking problem and during a "session" of heavy drinking would attack her with a knife. In some instances he was so riled by his "companion" that he would cut off pieces of his victim's skin, or cut out her internal organs. After attacking and killing heavy drinker, Tamara Sadikova, 70, in 2010, Martynov left two letters for police officials to find. He described the victim's son as a "nice man" who would no longer have to endure his alcoholic mother. After his detention in 2010, it was revealed that Martynov killed his victims because of a personal dislike for them.

Other murder victims included the killing of a man during a robbery, killing and dismembering an elderly woman in a forest and the rape and murder of another 70-year-old woman. Martynov is also believed to have committed violent crimes across at least 10 states across western and central Russia and numerous assaults.

Police were able to track down and arrest Martynov in November 2010, after he activated a mobile phone stolen from one of his victims. Martynov said that he wanted to be caught and did not resist the police efforts of his arrest. While awaiting his trial from his prison cell, Marytnov requested an inmate so that he could kill him to alleviate his boredom. He was convicted for eight murders and sentenced to life imprisonment, claiming he was motivated by the "cleaning of society".

Russia has a long history of serial killers, with many particularly disturbing stories. The Dnepropetrovsk Maniacs actually recorded themselves on a cell phone committing crimes, including beating people to death in 2007. One such video was posted online entitled "3 Guys 1 Hammer" and shows one of the victims, 48-year-old Sergei Yatzenko, being murdered by the gang – the video is extremely graphic. Between 2007-2008, investigators solved 132 murders in 11 serial killer cases but, since that time, Russia has registered more than 500 serial murders.

*LEFT: Vulnerable homeless people were the types of victims that Sergei Martynov would target*

# Alexander Pichushkin

Known as the "Chessboard Killer" (for the number of murders he wanted to commit) and the "Bitsevsky Park Maniac", where many of his victims were found, Alexander Pichushkin is thought to have had a macabre fascination with Andrei Chikatilo, Russia's notorious serial killer.

- - - - - - - - - - - - - - - - - - - - - - - - - - - - - - - - - - - - - - - - - -

**Pichushkin began killing in 1992, the same year that Chikatilo was convicted of his crimes, but he didn't become a serial killer until the following decade. Although he primarily targeted homeless men, he also killed a number of younger men, three women and a child in a "world" where he played "God", by deciding who would live and who would die.**

His preferred method of killing involved hitting his victims on the back of the head with a hammer – to avoid blood splashes on his clothes – but a number of his victims were also thrown alive into the sewer system below Bitsevsky Park. Those who died as a result of being hit with a hammer often had a bottle of vodka, his preferred method of luring the victims initially, stuck in their heads so that there was no chance of surviving. Pichushkin claimed that life without murder would be like "life without food", and that he was the "father" of all his victims because he: "...opened the door for them to another world". Despite his protestations, he was found sane by the Serbsky Institute psychiatric clinic.

When Pichushkin was 18, he killed the boyfriend of a neighbour whom he had fallen in love with. He spent many hours in Bitsevsky Park, a densely wooded area in the Moscow suburbs, popular with locals for relaxing with friends. Here he played chess with many opponents, whom he would invite for a drink of vodka after a game. Having persuaded his victims to accompany him to a secluded spot, he would then hit them over the head with the hammer – a method of killing that would last for five years until he was apprehended. Despite the fact that experts declared Pichushkin was deeply depressed following the death of his grandfather, and later his dog, he described his criminal activities as a "perpetual orgasm". He was a sadistic killer who had hammered stakes into the skull and around the eyes of one victim and who claimed at the time of his arrest that he would have killed time and time again had he not been caught. A metro ticket found on the body of his last victim, 36-year-old Marina Moskalyova, finally brought Pichushkin to justice. When CCTV footage of the woman's final movements were watched by police, it was Pichushkin that accompanied her along the metro platform.

It is estimated that he killed perhaps as many as 60 victims, which led to 15 years in solitary confinement at the start of his life sentence, for the murders of at least 49 people, when he was convicted in 2007.

*LEFT: Alexander Pichushkin looks on from a cell in a Moscow court room awaiting his sentence in October 2007*

# Guy Georges

Between 1991 and 1997, Guy Georges, also known as the "Beast of Bastille", stabbed seven women to death in Paris, France.

------------------------------------------------------------

**The narcissistic psychopath was sentenced to life imprisonment in 2001, without the possibility of parole, for 22 years following his arrest in 1998.**

Born in Angers, France in 1962, Georges was abandoned as a small child by his parents and taken in by the French welfare service. At the age of six, he was adopted into a family with 11 other adopted children. He didn't receive the love he needed and showed violent and aggressive behaviour from early on. His first attack, at the age of 14, was against his mentally disabled sister, Roselyne, whom he tried to strangle in 1976. In 1978, he was returned to the authorities after attacking another of his sisters, Christine. A year later, while in foster care, he attacked another girl. His foster family rejected him and he turned to alcohol. His next attack on a young woman came in 1980, followed by another the same month, where he knifed a girl in the face. Both girls survived their horrific ordeals.

He committed his first rape in 1981 at the age of 19. He had just moved to Paris after a year spent in prison in Angers. His victim was a neighbour whom he also stabbed and left for dead – incredibly, she survived. After a number of further attacks and short stints in prison for theft, Georges was sent to prison for 10 years in 1985. By the end of his sentence, while incarcerated at night, he was allowed out during the day, but in January 1991 he failed to return to prison. Instead, he travelled back to Paris where he followed 19-year-old student Pascale Escarfail. He raped the young woman, having forced his way into her apartment, before he slit her throat and watched her die. He calmly returned to prison a week later. He was eventually released in April 1992 and within weeks attacked another young woman. She escaped and Georges was arrested again.

Between January and the end of 1994, Georges had raped, tortured and murdered four women. A number of the attacks took place in the Bastille quarter to the east of Paris, earning him the nickname of the "Beast of Bastille". When Georges was eventually arrested in 1998, he was responsible for the brutal murders of seven young women, and attacks on many more. His arrest brought one of France's biggest manhunts in the country's criminal history to an end.

*ABOVE: Guy Georges's police mugshot from 1985*

*OPPOSITE: La Marmitiere residence where Guy Georges was placed after he attacked his two adopted sisters*

# Peter Tobin

Peter Tobin was always a problem child and, at only seven years old, he was sent to an approved school.

It seemed to have no effect and he would later spend time in both a young offender institution and prison. He had a string of failed marriages, with all three of his wives falling for his charming demeanour only to suffer later from his violent and sadistic nature.

In 1993, with his young son present, Tobin – born in Renfrewshire, Scotland in 1946 – held two young teenage girls hostage in his flat, forced them to drink alcohol then assaulted and raped them. Tobin fled, turning on the gas and leaving the two girls to die. Both survived, but not before Tobin hid with the Jesus Fellowship religious sect. He was later captured and sentenced to 14 years in prison. However, like his earlier incarcerations, this would not prevent him from offending again. What the authorities didn't know was that he already had two deaths to his name.

After serving 10 years of his sentence, Tobin was released in 2004 and, using an alias, he took a job as a handyman at St Patrick's Roman Catholic Church in Glasgow. Angelika Kluk, a 23-year-old student from Poland, was working at the church to help finance her studies. In 2006, Tobin attacked her, raping her and stabbing her before hiding her under the floorboards near the church's confessional. Horrifically, Angelika was still alive when Tobin buried her. Her bound and gagged body was found only a few days later and Tobin was arrested in London.

After his arrest for Angelika's murder, police began investigating Tobin for the 1991 murders of teenagers Vicky Hamilton and Dinah McNicol. Vicky had disappeared from a bus stop in Bathgate in February 1991. The case went cold until a knife with the young girl's DNA was discovered in Tobin's Edinburgh flat in 2007. A further search of Tobin's former residence at 50 Irvine Drive in Margate unearthed her remains beneath a sandpit in the back garden, along with those of another young woman. Dinah McNicol disappeared in August 1991 while hitch-hiking home from a music festival. After she vanished, large sums of money were withdrawn from her bank account, but no further leads could be found until her body was removed from the same sandpit.

It is possible that Tobin may have murdered even more women. The police have investigated Tobin in connection with dozens of murders and disappearances of teenage girls and there is even speculation that he is the notorious "Bible John", an unidentified serial killer who murdered three women from 1968-1969, after meeting them at the Barrowland Ballroom in Glasgow, Scotland. While there are similarities between physical descriptions of Bible John and Tobin and the modus operandi, DNA evidence from the Bible John murders is too degraded to provide any link.

Tobin is currently serving life in prison for the murders of Angelika Kluk, Vicky Hamilton and Dinah McNicol. He is a diagnosed psychopath who has never shown any remorse for his victims. Now a jail-cell recluse, he fears being attacked.

*ABOVE: Peter Tobin in November 2007 at Linlithgow Sheriff Court in connection with the murder of Vicky Hamilton, who went missing in 1991*

*OPPOSITE: Police officers and forensic archaeologists continue their search and investigation outside the Tobin's former house*

# Joel Rifkin

Reacting to the mistreatment he had suffered at the hands of others, Joel Rifkin sought solace in his own disturbed world of dark fantasy.

- - - - - - - - - - - - - - - - - - - - - - - - - - - - - - - - - - - - - - - - - - - - - - - - - -

**He became obsessed by the film "Frenzy" by Alfred Hitchcock, and was consumed by the concept of strangling prostitutes. Unaware of their son's dark desires, his parents gave him a car. He used this vehicle to pick up women working the streets. He spent every penny he had on prostitutes and eventually had to drop out of college.**

Joel David Rifkin was born in 1959 in the USA and given up for adoption. His adoptive parents, Benjamin and Jeanne Rifkin, welcomed baby Joel into their home in New York when he was just three weeks old.

An isolated, bullied teenager, Rifkin tried his hand at many professions, but developed a particular passion for horticulture. He then worked as a groundsman, a horticulturist and as a self-employed landscaper.

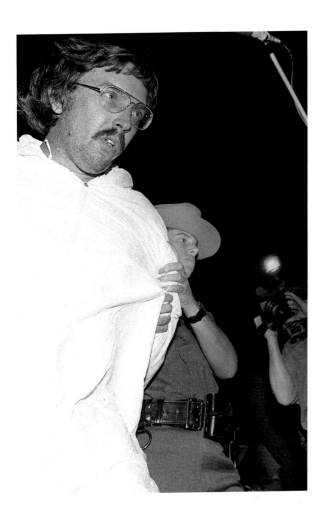

In March 1989, unable to control his Frenzy-inspired fantasies any longer, Rifkin abducted a young sex worker called "Susie", took her to his home, and clubbed her with a Howitzer artillery shell. She survived the savage beating so he strangled her to death. Rifkin butchered her corpse with a craft knife. To hide her identity he cut off her fingertips, and pulled out her teeth with pliers before placing her severed head in an empty paint tin. He threw "Susie's" arms and torso into New York's East River, and hid her legs and head on a golf course.

Several days passed before a member of the Hopewell Valley Golf Club made a horrifying discovery – "Susie's" head in the paint tin. Investigating police officers were unable to identify the victim, and found no clues that might identify the perpetrator of the murder.

On 28th June 1993, State Troopers attempted to stop Rifkin's truck having spotted him driving along the Southern State Parkway without registration plates. There followed a high-speed pursuit, which ended when Rifkin crashed his truck into a telegraph pole outside the Mineola courthouse. The Troopers noticed a horrible smell emanating from the back of the truck and after searching the vehicle discovered the rotting corpse of Tiffany Bresciani, a 22-year-old prostitute.

Police officers then began a detailed investigation of the house Rifkin shared with his elderly mother, Jeanne, and his sister. Here they found trophies from his victims including handbags, purses, diaries, jewellery, bras and knickers. Stacked beside his bed were books on serial killers. When they searched his garage, they found a chainsaw with blood and dismembered flesh hanging from it. Sometimes he had killed the women at home, sometimes in his car. He dismembered them on a makeshift table or in the bathtub. Rifkin had committed his first murder in 1989, and over the following four years is believed to have murdered and dismembered a further 16 women, making him New York's most prolific killer.

Rifkin was convicted on nine counts of second-degree murder, and sentenced to 203 years in prison. He will become eligible for parole on 26th February 2197.

*LEFT: Joel Rifkin is transferred to a holding cell after being charged with second-degree murder*

*OPPOSITE: A plane lands in the background as police investigate a body dumped by Rifkin in a remote area of JFK Airport*

# Tsutomu Miyazaki

Teased as a "nerd" ("otaku" in Japanese slang), Tsutomu Miyazaki had an unhealthy obsession with video games, anime, manga and computers in general.

- - - - - - - - - - - - - - - - - - - - - - - - - - - - - - - - - - - - - - - - - - -

**When he was arrested in 1989 for obscene acts, it was discovered he already had a collection of more than 5,750 videotapes including slasher movies and torture porn, as well photos of his victims. He also possessed the "Guinea Pig" film series, as well as "Mermaid in a Manhole", which was considered one of the goriest movies ever made at the time.**

The influences in Mayazaki's life, including the fact that both his sisters found him repulsive, led him to become the "Little Girl Murderer", also dubbed the "Otaku Killer" and the "Cannibal Nerd". He was a sadist, fetishist, cannibal and serial killer who murdered four little girls aged between four and seven years old in Saitama Prefecture, Japan. His four victims included Mari Konno, 7, Masami Yoshizawa, 7, Erika Nanba, 4, and Ayako Nomoto, 5.

Born with deformed hands, fused from the wrist down, Miyazaki was ostracised and bullied from a young age but it was these hands that he would later use in his brutal killings of four children. His pattern involved luring the young girls into his car before taking them to a secluded spot where they would be photographed. Each victim was then strangled and killed, disrobed and sexually assaulted before the killer then kept their clothes.

The final victim, five-year-old Ayako Nomoto was taken to Miyazaki's home where he videotaped her body and drank her blood. In a horrific move, he then ate the little girl's hands. In a macabre twist, Miyazaki would phone the victim's families and then remain silent at the other end of the phone. When the families ignored him, he would let the phone ring and ring, before sending them horrific postcards with letters cut from magazines spelling out words such as "death". The Konno family received a box that contained photographs of their missing child's clothing, teeth and charred pieces of bone.

Miyazaki was eventually caught when he lured a little girl away from her sister. The other child fled for help and he was caught photographing the abducted child's genitals by her father, who called the police. He was caught quickly and readily confessed to the murders. While his mother visited him regularly in prison, his father was so distraught at what his son had become that he committed suicide not long after Miyazaki's arrest.

For 20 years, after he was convicted and the death sentence was passed, there were various attempts to convince the courts that the serial killer was insane.

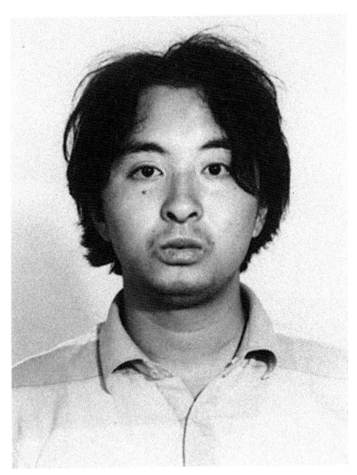

*ABOVE: Tsutomu Miyazaki was sentenced to death by Toyko District Court in April 1997 for the gruesome killings of four young girls*

*ABOVE: Tsutomu Miyazaki (second left) with police
officers at a murder site in October 1989*

In addition, Miyazaki claimed that his alter ego "Rat Man" was
ultimately responsible for the murders. While some experts declared
he suffered from multiple personality disorder, others argued he was
perfectly sane and should suffer the death penalty for his heinous
crimes. On 17th June 2008, Miyazaki faced the hangman's noose
and, for the majority, an evil serial killer was finally brought to justice.

# Charles Cullen

Charles Cullen, the "Angel of Death", was a nurse who once chillingly claimed: "I thought I was helping", following his 11 consecutive life sentences given in 2006 for the murder of at least 40 patients in his care.

- - - - - - - - - - - - - - - - - - - - - - - - - - - - - - - - - - - - - - - - - - -

**However, Cullen had worked with patients for 16 years before his crimes came to light and it is believed that the death toll could reach as many as 400. Today, Cullen is the most prolific serial killer in American history.**

The former nurse claimed that he was ending the "suffering" of patients, but many of those who died at his hands were in hospital for routine operations and procedures. His youngest victim was 21-year-old Michael T Strenko, who was admitted to hospital for routine spleen surgery whom Cullen poisoned. He had been fired or asked to move on from five hospitals before he landed a job at St. Luke's University Hospital in Bethlehem, Pennsylvania.

The suspicions that his former employers had with regard to his activities and work ethics were never noted on Cullen's file and he was free to find new employment when a job didn't work out. The serial killer admitted that had he never been caught, the killings would have continued. He admitted to the deaths of five patients while working at St Luke's (there had been suspicions about his practices and he was asked to resign). He moved on to Somerset Medical Centre, New Jersey, where he admitted to killing 13 patients by lethal injection over 13 months. The death of Florian Gall, a Roman Catholic priest, began a chain of events that would lead to Cullen's arrest.

By this time, staff realised that Cullen was making visits to patients, to whom he was not assigned, and administering drugs, without consent. The hospital strongly suspected Cullen was killing patients, informed police and fired him on 31st October 2003. He was kept under police surveillance while investigations were ongoing and was finally arrested in December that same year. He agreed to co-operate with the authorities if the death sentence was not sought. He is currently serving a life sentence, without parole, of over 100 years.

*BELOW: St Luke's Hospital in Bethlehem, where Charles Cullen worked as a nurse*

*OPPOSITE: Cullen listens to the charges in a courtroom in Somerville, New Jersey, in December 2003*

# Anatoly Onoprienko

When Anatoly Onoprienko was four years old, his mother died and he was sent to live in an orphanage, but his older brother stayed with his father. By the age of seven, Onoprienko was already hearing voices.

------------------------------------------------

**Anatoly Onoprienko reacted badly to his father's rejection of him in favour of his older brother and his youthful resentment grew into a murderous, destructive, adult rage against the very concept of "family".**

Onoprienko – born in the city of Laski, Ukraine, in 1956 – would select an isolated house, and then cause a distraction to attract the attention of its occupants. During the confusion, he killed the oldest adult male, followed by his wife – and all the children. Sometimes he shot the children, sometimes he chopped them to death with an axe as they pleaded for mercy. He then searched the house for valuables, and set it on fire to destroy any evidence.

During one home invasion, Onoprienko discovered a little girl cowering on her bed, praying. She had watched him kill both her parents. Seconds before he beat her to death, he asked her to tell him where her parents hid their money. She looked at him with angry eyes and said: "No, I won't". Onoprienko later admitted that he admired her strength but claimed to have felt nothing as he bludgeoned her to death.

He claimed he had been following "kill" commands received inside his head, like a Terminator robot and he spoke at length about his crimes. "To me killing is like ripping up a duvet ... Men, women, old people, children, they're all just the same. I have never felt sorry for those I killed. No love, no hatred, just blind indifference. I don't see them as individuals, just as masses.

"To me it was like hunting people down. I would be sitting, bored, with nothing to do. And then suddenly this idea would get into my head. I would do everything I could to get it out of my mind, but I couldn't. It was stronger than me. So I would get in the car or catch a train and go out to kill.

"If I am ever let out, I will start killing again. But this time it will be ten times worse. I am being groomed to serve Satan. After what I have learnt out there, I have no competitors in my field. And if I am not killed I will escape from this jail and the first thing I'll do is find Kuchma [the Ukrainian president] and hang him from a tree by his testicles."

In 1996, police captured Yury Mozola, aged 26, whom they suspected had committed at least seven of the "Terminator" murders. Over six days, Mozola was tortured to death. Seventeen days after his death, Onoprienko, the actual murderer, was captured and charged.

Anatoly Onoprienko – the "Beast of Ukraine" – was convicted of 52 counts of murder, and was sentenced to life imprisonment. He died, aged 54, of heart failure in Zhytomyr Prison, Ukraine on 17th August 2013.

*LEFT: An unrepentant Anatoly Onoprienko*

# José Antonio Rodriguez Vega

José Antonio Rodriguez Vega became known as "The Old Lady Killer" after he raped and murdered at least 16 elderly women in and around Santander, Spain, between August 1987 and April 1988.

**He was born on 3rd December 1957 and grew up with a terminally ill father, whom he beat regularly. After discovering that her son was beating his own father, and having coped with other acts of violence, Vega was eventually thrown out of the family home by his mother.**

José Antonio Rodriguez Vega started his criminal career when he began raping women "in revenge" against his mother whom he hated for throwing him out. On 17th October 1979, he was arrested for his crimes and was sentenced to 27 years imprisonment. However, Rodriguez Vega demonstrated good behaviour while in prison and only served eight years after the sentence was reduced.

When he was released, his wife divorced him but he soon remarried and his second wife, a mentally disabled woman, was subjected to torture and humiliation at the hands of her husband. However, those around him were not aware of his frightening and disturbing behaviour as Rodriguez Vega managed to keep up the charade of a happy marriage and was generally seen as a hard-working, caring individual and good husband. The domestic violence that his wife suffered was suffered in silence and ignorance.

Rodriguez Vega targeted his first murder victim on 6th August 1987 when he entered the home of 82-year-old Margarita Gonzàlez. He forced her to swallow her own false teeth before raping and suffocating her to death. A further 15 women were brutally killed by Rodriguez Vega before his capture on 21st January 1988. At his arrest, he confessed to the murders but later changed his story during the trial, claiming the women died from natural causes. He displayed anti-social behaviour and was eventually diagnosed as a psychopath. He charmed his victims to gain their trust, usually on the pretence of helping with jobs in or around the house, so entry into their homes was easy. Once inside he would attack his victims by strangling or suffocating them. Although the attacks were sexually driven, no trace of semen was ever found on the victims and the vicious killer left each elderly lady in her own bed to give the illusion that she had died of old age in her sleep.

Described as a cold and calculating individual who took souvenirs from each attack, which ranged from a plastic bouquet of flowers to a television set, Vega displayed the "trophies" in a room at his home, which police discovered during his arrest. In 1992, he was sentenced to 440 years imprisonment which, according to the Spanish judicial system, meant he would only serve 20 years.

On 24th October 2002, two inmates attacked Vega while he walked through the prison grounds and the wounds they inflicted led to his death. He was buried the following day.

*ABOVE: José Antonio Rodríguez Vega being escorted by a police officer*

# Richard Angelo

Richard Angelo grew up with two parents working in the education sector. After graduating from thc St. John the Baptist Diocesan High School in 1980, he went on to the Farmingdale State College to study nursing.

**Angelo found employment at the Good Samaritan Hospital in the 1980s where he fantasised about being recognised as a hero. His burning ambition led him to poison in excess of 35 patients in his care in order to bring them close to death.**

Richard Angelo, born in 1962, would wait until patients went into cardiac arrest and then attempt to save their lives. However, on many occasions he was unsuccessful in saving these victims and the resultant deaths led to multiple murders.

His modus operandi involved administering a combination of Pavulon and Anectine into patient's IV tubes. Pavulon is a muscle relaxant and is one of three drugs used for lethal injection in the United States. Anectine is the drug commonly used in hospitals to induce short-term paralysis and muscle relaxation when performing tracheal intubation.

During the course of his twisted hero-seeking activities, Angelo poisoned more than 35 victims, 25 of whom died when he failed to "save" them. On 11th October 1986, colleagues grew suspicious of Angelo when Gerolamo Kucich, a 73-year-old patient, used the call button to attract the assistance of another nurse. He complained that he felt unwell after receiving an injection and went on to describe Angelo's profile as "heavy-set with a dark beard and glasses". After a urine sample was analysed, it was discovered that Kucich tested positive to having received Pavulon and Anectin, neither of which were officially prescribed to him. Vials of both drugs were found at Angelo's home and in his locker at the hospital before he was subsequently arrested.

At his arraignment, the judge refused to set bail for the 25-year-old Angelo, saying the man may be responsible for the "largest series of mass murders in the metropolitan area, if not the country."

He admitted to having administered the drugs to previous patients, which led to nearly 30 bodies being exhumed and tested for the drug. As a result, it was discovered that Angelo killed at least 10 patients during a seven-month period.

During the trial, psychologists testified that Angelo had a dissociative identity disorder, a condition that left him unaware of his actions as he was acting under a multiple personality. However, two psychiatric experts that assessed Angelo disagreed that it was dissociative identity disorder and determined that instead he had a personality disorder and was well aware of his actions.

Angelo was found guilty of two counts of second-degree murder, second-degree manslaughter and six counts of assault. He was sentenced to 61 years imprisonment.

*LEFT: Richard Angelo is led into court to be arraigned in November 1987*

# Angel Reséndiz

Angel Reséndiz was abused physically by his mother and aged six was sent to live with an uncle, who raped him and who allowed him to be raped, yet again, by a local paedophile.

------------------------------------------------------------

**At the age of 11, Reséndiz ran away from home, lived on the streets and took up glue sniffing. Aged 16 he made repeated illegal attempts to cross the Mexican border and enter Texas, in the United States.**

Eventually Reséndiz – born on 1st August 1959, in Izúcar de Matamoros, Mexico – slipped across the border and, in 1988, lived for a while in St. Louis. He combined working with burglary, theft and assault. He established a pattern: offend, get caught, go to prison, get deported back to Mexico, then return to the US. This repeat offending saw Reséndiz spend a total of 11 years inside US jails.

In 1986, Reséndiz committed his first murders in Mexico when he killed a homeless woman and her Cuban boyfriend. Five years later, Reséndiz killed his first American. Michael White was beaten to death with a house brick in Kentucky. Over the following eight years, Reséndiz is known to have killed a further 12 people.

As his modus operandi became established, Reséndiz was christened "The Railroad Killer" because all his kills were committed near railway tracks. In June 1999, Reséndiz was named on the FBI's list of Ten Most Wanted Fugitives. A reward of $125,000 was offered for his capture.

Reséndiz jumped trains and crossed the land borders between Mexico, the United States and Canada. Being so mobile, and having no fixed address, he found it easy to evade capture. Reséndiz identified his victims at random while travelling on the trains, targeting men, although some women were attacked and raped. But these sexual attacks were secondary as robbery was his primary goal.

Reséndiz would follow his victims to their homes and murder them, using any blunt object that came to hand as his murder weapon – rocks, bricks, even a pick axe. Once the victim was dead, Reséndiz would eat their food and search their homes for valuables and personal documentation – he was curious about the lives of his victims. He stole cash, jewellery and other valuables, and presented them to his wife, Julieta Dominguez Reyes, who was living in Mexico. Having killed a victim, Reséndiz would cover the corpse or hide it from view, but made no attempt to bury it.

An investigative breakthrough was made when Drew Carter, a Texas Ranger, contacted Reséndiz's sister, Manuela, who was living in Albuquerque, New Mexico. Carter promised, in writing, that if she helped him capture Reséndiz, her brother would be guaranteed safety in prison, he would be granted regular visits from family

members, and he would receive psychological care. Consequently, Angel Reséndiz met Carter, and surrendered to US law enforcement officers.

However, Reséndiz was charged with, and convicted of, first-degree murder. He was sentenced to death by lethal injection and the sentence was carried out on 27th June 2006, in Huntsville, Texas.

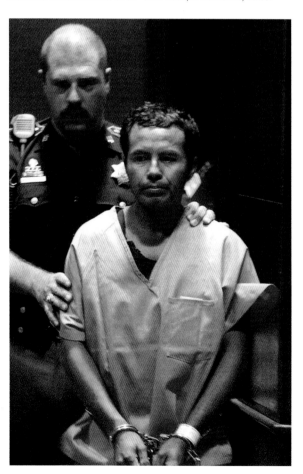

*ABOVE: Angel Reséndiz is led into District Court in Houston, Texas, in July 1999*

# Kenneth Erskine

Kenneth Erskine was abandoned by his parents at a young age. He became a vagrant and solvent abuser and his criminal career started with minor burglaries.

- - - - - - - - - - - - - - - - - - - - - - - - - - - - - - - - - - - - - - - - - - -

**At the age of 18, Erskine stabbed his boyfriend at the time. However, for various reasons, he was not charged with the attack and was freed from police custody. The nature of his crimes soon intensified when Erskine began breaking into the homes of the elderly where he would then conduct acts of sexual assault and murder.**

During 1986, Kenneth Erskine is known to have sexually assaulted and strangled seven elderly residents in their homes but is suspected of four further murders.

Erskine – born in Hammersmith, London in July 1963 – would seek opportunities to enter a property through unsecured or open windows. After gaining entry, Erskine would quickly force his victim to the floor and kneel on their chest, using his body weight to secure them beneath him. His left hand would be used to cover the mouth of his victim while he used his right hand to grasp at the throat, strangling them to death. Four of the pensioners had been sodomised, however it remains unclear whether the sexual nature of the attacks had occurred before or after the victims had been murdered.

His first attack was on a 78-year-old woman living in Wandsworth in London. Eileen Emms was raped and murdered in her flat on 9th April 1986. Two months later, the "Stockwell Strangler" – as Erskine was dubbed – struck again when 67-year-old Janet Cockett was found strangled on 9th June. A palm print was forensically discovered on a window at the scene of the crime, which later would lead to the successful identification of the killer.

Erskine had demonstrated bisexual tendencies through the sexual assault and molestation of both men and women. On 28th June, Polish pensioners and World War II veterans Valentine Glime (aged 84) and Zbigniew Stabawa (aged 94) were subjected to his vile and perverted attacks when they were sexually assaulted and strangled in a residential home in Stockwell.

Erskine was arrested on 28th July after he was discovered trying to conceal a savings account from social security. Upon his arrest, his palm print was then linked to the earlier crime scene at Janet Cockett's residence. At a police line-up, he was identified by a 74-year-old witness whom Erskine had attacked earlier that month.

When questioned in court, Erskine said he couldn't remember the murders and was seen to be masturbating during the trial. He was found guilty of murder and received life imprisonment with a 40-year minimum term. In 2006, he was transported to the notorious

Broadmoor Hospital after medical reassessment and diagnosis suggested chronic schizophrenia and antisocial personality disorder. His murder convictions were reduced to manslaughter when he appealed on the grounds of diminished responsibility as a result of his mental instability in 2009. In April 2016, Erskine moved again, to Thornford Park Hospital, Thatcham, Berkshire.

*ABOVE: Kenneth Erskine arrives at Southwestern Magistrates' Court to face charges in connection with the "Stockwell Strangler" case*

# Richard Ramirez

Growing up during the turbulent Vietnam War era, young Richard Ramirez was heavily influenced by his older cousin, Mike, a disturbed Vietnam War veteran.

**Mike would boast to his cousin about the murders and mutilations he performed during the war, even showing the 12-year-old boy polaroid pictures of his victims, including photos of him raping women.**

When he was 13, Ramirez was smoking marijuana when his cousin Mike and his wife got into an argument. Mike pulled out his gun and shot her in the face, killing her in front of Ramirez. It was a fatal incident that would later fuel Ramirez's own crime spree.

From April 1984 to August 1985, Ramirez terrorised the greater Los Angeles and San Francisco areas while on a home invasion terror spree. His first victim was a nine-year-old girl who was found in a hotel basement in April 1984. His second was a 79-year-old woman who was stabbed to death in her sleep so viciously that she was nearly decapitated. Ramirez gained public attention and was dubbed "The Night Stalker," "The Walk-In Killer" and "The Valley Intruder" after he went on a multi-victim spree on 17th March 1985. He shot 22-year-old Maria Hernandez in the face as she was arriving home then went inside the house and murdered her room-mate. An hour later, he murdered another woman by pulling her from her car and shooting her twice.

The summer of 1985 saw Ramirez at his most brutal. The confessed Satanist broke into multiple homes, beat his victims and ordered them to hand over all their valuables or brutally murdered them. He would murder the husbands quickly, often shooting them, then rape and sodomise the wives. He then bludgeoned his female victims with hammers, shocked them with electrical cords, bound them in handcuffs and hacked them with machetes. He performed a post-mortem mutilation on at least one elderly woman, gouging out her eyes and storing them in a jewellery box. Prior to a hideous death when he forced the women to retrieve their valuables, he would make them "swear on Satan" that they weren't hiding anything from him. He also used lipstick to scrawl pentagons on their legs and on the walls.

He was eventually apprehended when a thumbprint on a stolen car linked to "The Night Stalker" matched Ramirez's police profile. His mug shot, from previous burglary arrests, was broadcast nationwide. The next day, he was spotted near Los Angeles and an angry mob surrounded him and beat him. He would have been killed had it not been for the intervention of the police.

Ramirez was found guilty on 33 counts of murder, five of attempted murder, 11 sexual assaults and 14 burglaries. He was sentenced to death by gas chamber. While awaiting his execution, he amassed dozens of fans and even married one, freelance magazine editor Doreen Lioy, who first wrote to him after his arrest. Ramirez and Lioy eventually separated, but Ramirez was engaged a second time. He died of complications from lymphoma in June 2013.

*RIGHT: Serial killer Richard Ramirez aka "The Night Stalker" in his booking photo in December 1984 in Los Angeles, California*

# Gary Leon Ridgway

Gary Ridgway's mother Mary dominated her family and arguments between her and her husband Thomas were frequent and bitter. These arguments disrupted the childhoods of the Ridgways's three boys: Gary, Gregory and Thomas junior.

---

**Gary Ridgway became a bed-wetter. His mother would discover an "accident", rip the blankets from the bed and strip Ridgway, humiliating and belittling him in the process. Perhaps in consequence, Ridgway developed conflicting emotions about his mother; intense anger and sexual attraction.**

Gary Ridgway was born on 18th February 1949, in Salt lake City, Utah, and experienced a troubled adolescence. Possessing an IQ of 82, he struggled at school. Aged 16, Ridgway knifed a six-year-old boy in the liver because he had: "...wondered what it would be like to kill someone." Fortunately, the child survived the attack.

Ridgway graduated from high school, married his girlfriend, Claudia Barrows, and was drafted into the US Navy. Serving on a supply ship, he experienced combat in the Vietnam War but, off duty, Ridgway indulged his sexual appetite with local prostitutes. Preferring unprotected sex, he caught gonorrhoea. Catching a disease angered Ridgway, but he kept paying for sexual services and still refused to wear a condom. While Ridgway served in Vietnam, 19-year-old Claudia had an affair and, a year later, Ridgway's first marriage ended in divorce.

Ridgway remarried and found religion. He read the Bible aloud in his place of work – the Kenworth Truck Factory, Renton, Washington State, and at home. What he read moved him to tears on many occasions. His second wife, Marcia, was required to live a moral and pious home life, according to the strict teachings of their church minister, and yet the sexually ravenous Ridgway continued to seek prostitutes for carnal release. Ridgway insisted that Marcia should have sex with him in inappropriate, public places so needless to say his second marriage also ended in divorce.

Ridgway appears to have been addicted to sex. Sex with different partners, sex in public places and sex several times a day. He seemingly appeared to be torn between his faith and his insatiable lust for women's naked bodies.

Ridgway began to kill young women in 1982. He abducted prostitutes and runaway girls, took them to his house, strangled them – with his hands or a ligature – then dumped their corpses in remote, wooded areas. Ridgway then returned to have sex with the decomposing corpses. The bodies of his first victims were discovered beside the Green River – hence his nickname – "The Green River Killer".

It was forensic DNA evidence which finally trapped Ridgway in 2001 and identified him as the Green River Killer. He was charged with four counts of aggravated murder in December 2001 but confessed to killing 48 women between 1982 and 2001.

To escape the death penalty, Ridgway entered a plea bargain and confessed to a further 12 murders, while disclosing the locations of four undiscovered women's corpses in return for life imprisonment. His plea bargain was accepted in December 2003. He continues to serve his life sentence without any possibility of parole.

*LEFT: Investigators search for the remains of one of Gary Leon Ridgway's victims*

*OPPOSITE: Ridgway cries in a King County Washington Superior Court in December 2003 as he faces the families of some of his victims*

# Robert Black

During questioning, it was apparent that Robert Black, despite claiming to love children, merely saw the young girls he kidnapped as playthings to be explored until he no longer had a use for them.

------------------------------------------------------

**In 2011, a jury heard how serial killer Robert Black had already been convicted of killing three young girls, abducting another and attempting to snatch a fifth victim while on trial for the kidnap, sexual assault and murder of Jennifer Cardy in County Antrim in August 1981. While Black had given investigators an insight into his mind and patterns of killings, he had not actually confessed to any of his crimes.**

At the time of his 10 summonses in 1992, including three for the murders of Sarah Harper, 10, Susan Maxwell, 11, and five-year-old Caroline Hogg, Black implied to police that the breakup of his one and only real relationship with Pamela Hodgson was the driving force behind his crimes. However, Black was known to have had a long history of sexual deviancy, which began at an early age, while his abnormal propensity for targeting pre-pubescent girls provided strong evidence of his guilt. After his arrest in 1990, Black was found in the possession of children's clothing and images of children being abused, while searches of his van which he drove around the country on deliveries had rags and tape inside. He told police that he wore the children's clothing, including a swimming costume for a girl aged eight to 10. In frank admissions, he also described how, from the age of eight, he had pushed things up his anus – photographs of Black with a wine bottle and another with a table leg inside his anus were taken away by police. What Black really fantasised about was genitalia; sickeningly, he was particularly obsessed with little girls.

*ABOVE: Jennifer Cardy, aged 9*

At the age of 12, he attempted his first rape on a young girl with whom he failed to have sexual intercourse. He forced her to lie there while he removed her underwear and touched her, along with two other boys. By the time he was 17, Black had become a sexual predator and abducted a seven-year-old girl on the pretext of showing her some kittens. As Black held the child to the ground with his hand around her throat, the girl lost consciousness. He then performed explicit acts on her unconscious body while masturbating. By 1966, Black's sexual obsession with little girls had grown into something significantly sinister and, during the 1970s, he discovered a penchant for magazines advocating child pornography. More than 100 of these publications were found in his possession at the time of his arrest.

*ABOVE: Sarah Harper, aged 10*

*ABOVE: Robert Black*

By the time police held an emergency crisis summit in London in 1986, Sarah Harper's body had already been found in the River Trent in Nottingham in April that year. It was later confirmed that she had been violently sexually assaulted and thrown – still alive – into the river around Junction 24 of the M1 after going missing from close to her home in Morley, Leeds, the previous month. She wasn't the only child on the police list at the summit and senior officers believed that they were seeking a man, or group of men, responsible for the abduction, sexual assault, killing and disposing of children. Sarah's death was eventually linked to that of 11-year-old Susan Maxwell, found murdered in July 1982 and five-year-old Caroline Hogg,

murdered in July 1983 when it emerged all three had suffered sexual assaults. By following the delivery routes Black had taken, police pieced together evidence to convict him of all three murders.

Black's trial saw him plead guilty to the abduction and assault of a young girl in August 1990. He was sentenced to life imprisonment. Black refused to admit to the murders of Susan, Caroline and Sarah but he was found guilty of all three murders in May 1994. In January 2016, Black died of natural causes in Maghaberry Prison, Northern Ireland.

# Michael Ross

Michael Bruce Ross was born in Putnam, Connecticut, in 1959, where he grew up on a chicken farm and landed the gruesome job of strangling the fowl.

**Ross's mother took a lover and ran away from her husband and son to be with him. She returned home, only to be admitted to Norwich Hospital, Connecticut, with thoughts of suicide and beating her children.**

She was released from hospital and returned home, where she began abusing all four of her children, with Ross bearing the brunt of his mother's rage. A babysitting uncle may also have sexually abused Ross as a young child, but he committed suicide when the boy was just six-years-old.

Ross had exhibited signs of antisocial behaviour from an early age. He was an intelligent child with an IQ of 122, and he got good marks at school. Eventually, in 1977, he went to study agricultural economics at Cornell University. As a first-year student, Ross dated a female student. She became pregnant and had an abortion, and their relationship failed. At about the same time, Ross started developing violent sexual fantasies about women, which became more and more powerful and compelling.

By his second-year at Cornell, Ross was stalking a number of women and found himself in the grip of overwhelming sexual urges. By his final year, he had committed his first rape, and his first rape and murder by strangulation. Horrified by what he had done, he decided to kill himself, but was unable to enact his plan. He made a vow that he would never hurt anyone again. However Ross was unable to keep his promise when his inner "voices" became too strong. By 1984, Ross had raped and murdered a further seven women aged between 14-25.

As the body count mounted, the police assigned Michael Malchic to head the investigation. The final murder victim, Wendy Baribeault, had been abducted by the driver of a blue Toyota car. Police interviewed all the local owners of Toyota cars until they reached Ross. While being questioned, he dropped Malchic hints that he was the perpetrator. As questioning continued, the two men developed a rapport, and eventually, in June 1984, Ross confessed to abducting, raping and murdering eight women.

At his trial, Ross again confessed to the murder and rape of eight women. On 6th July 1987, Ross was convicted on all counts, and sentenced to death and spent 18 years on Death Row awaiting his execution.

During his incarceration Ross was a model inmate. He became a devout Roman Catholic, acted as a "big brother" to younger prisoners, and he learnt to read Braille. Although he had opposed the death penalty, in the final year of his imprisonment Ross grew to welcome his impending death. He believed he had been forgiven by God, and would go to a better place. He waived his right to a final appeal for clemency, he said, to spare the families of his victims further legal trials. On 13th May 2005, Michael Ross, was executed by lethal injection at the Osborn Correctional Institution, Somers, Connecticut.

*LEFT: Anti-death penalty protesters keep vigil outside the Osborn Correctional Institution after the execution of convicted serial killer Michael Ross, Connecticut's first in 45 years*

# Robert Hansen

The son of a domineering father, Robert Hansen grew up a quiet loner. Hansen's severe acne and disabling stammer made him a natural target for school bullies.

---

**Shunned by pretty girls at school, he developed cruel revenge fantasies, which he would act out in later life. Hansen descended into petty crime and was imprisoned for setting fire to a school bus garage. After his release, he moved to Anchorage, Alaska and reinvented himself in the wild expanses before going on to earn the nickname the "Alaskan Serial Killer".**

Robert Hansen (born in Iowa, in the US) set up as a baker, took flying lessons and bought his own private aircraft. Being one of the "lads" in an enthusiastic gun-toting community suited Hansen ideally. Respected as a skilled outdoor man, Hansen stalked wolves and bears with rifles or bow and arrows. He became a hunting champion and even set a number of records.

In 1977, he was diagnosed with bipolar disorder and prescribed lithium but his unpredictable mood swings, despite the medication, continued with fatal consequences. Hansen began to enact his revenge fantasies. Between 1971 and 1983, he abducted and murdered 17 women and raped 30 others.

He flew women out into the Alaskan wilderness and forced them to act out his darkest sexual fantasies. Depending upon how well they performed, Hansen would either fly them home or murder them. Often, he would strip the women naked and "hunt" them like prey through the wilderness. He would "make the kill" with a high-powered rifle or a hunting knife.

In 1983, 17-year-old Cindy Paulson managed to escape from Hansen and, after a terrifying pursuit, was carried to safety by a passing truck driver. She told police officers that Hansen had offered her $200 for oral sex but, when she got into his car, he pulled a gun and drove her to his home. He chained her by the neck to a post in the basement while he tortured, raped and assaulted her. Next he planned to fly her to his isolated cabin deep in the Alaskan wilderness but Cindy, though handcuffed, managed to break free.

Hansen denied all Cindy's accusations, claiming that she was trying to extort money from him. His lies were further strengthened by a false alibi from a friend and he was released without charge.

The corpses of three murdered women were then discovered outside Anchorage. The FBI provided a psychological profile of the perpetrator: an experienced hunter with low self-esteem, a history of rejection by women, a collector of "souvenirs", or "hunting trophies" from his kills. The killer might have a stammer.

At last, a search warrant was issued for Hansen's home, cars and aircraft. Police found jewellery taken from the missing women, many firearms, and an aviation map showing kill locations – leading to Hansen's arrest.

Damning ballistics and the aviation map evidence ensured that Hansen was convicted for his heinous crimes. He was sentenced to serve life, plus 461 years in prison. He was held in the Spring Hill Correctional Centre, in Seward, Alaska.

In August 2014, Hansen died of natural causes.

*RIGHT: Robert Hansen with the horns from a record Dall sheep he killed*

# Jeffrey Dahmer

Known as the "Milwaukee Cannibal", Jeffrey Dahmer was a notorious sex offender and serial killer responsible for the deaths of 17 men and boys.

**Born in 1960, Dahmer raped, murdered and dismembered his victims and later in his crimes turned to necrophilia and cannibalism. In 1992, he was sentenced to 15 terms of life imprisonment for 15 of the murders. Two years later, he was found beaten to death by a fellow inmate at Columbia Correctional Institution.**

On 22nd July 1991, two Milwaukee police officers stopped Tracy Edwards, whom they found wandering the streets at midnight with one wrist in a handcuff. They questioned Edwards and discovered that the man had escaped from a "weird dude" who had handcuffed him in an apartment and threatened him with a knife. The police decided to investigate. Apartment 213, in the Oxford Apartments, revealed a shocking discovery.

It was the same apartment that two months earlier police had returned Konerak, the "drunk" 19-year-old homosexual lover of Dahmer, who had been found running around the streets naked. Local residents had tried to intervene and persuade the police that Konerak was just a child and terrified of blond Dahmer, but police chose to believe the story of the 31-year-old and returned his "lover" to his care. What they failed to realise was that Konerak was just 14 years old, stupefied with the drugs he'd been forced to take and running for his life. They also failed to register that the extremely bad smell in the neat apartment came from the three-day old rotting corpse of Tony Hughes, whom Dahmer had already murdered. Dahmer strangled Konerak once the police had gone and had sex with the boy's corpse. Dahmer then took photos of the dead boy, dismembered his body and cleaned and kept the skull as a trophy.

Inside the apartment, police found photos of dismembered bodies, skulls and a severed head in the fridge. They also found three more skulls in the freezer and, while he appeared calm to begin with, Dahmer fought the two police officers when they tried to cuff him. He was eventually overwhelmed and taken into custody. It was then that the true horrors of his crimes came to light.

The apartment contained photos of Dahmer's victims, prior to death, in various erotic and bondage poses, and investigators also found a metal pot containing decomposing hands and a penis. The genitalia of a number of males was also found preserved in formaldehyde in a cupboard, while chloroform was discovered in another closet.

Eventually, Dahmer confessed to his 13-year killing spree and named a hitch-hiker he had picked up, Steve Hicks, as his first victim in 1978. Dahmer had been having fantasies about killing men and having sex with their corpses for four years at the time of Hicks's death. By 1987, the pattern of picking up young men in gay bars and luring them with the promise of money or beer in return for some photos was established. Dahmer found eating human flesh gave him an erection and believed that by eating his victims, they came alive again, in him.

*LEFT: Number 213 at the Oxford Apartments where police found the remains of 11 of Jeffrey Dahmer's victims*

*OPPOSITE: Jeffrey Dahmer in the courtroom of Milwaukee Circuit Court in July 1991*

# Andrei Chikatilo

Born in the Ukraine, in 1936, not long after the Ukrainian famine, Andrei Chikatilo was brought up on the story his mother told of how his older brother had been killed and eaten by the neighbours because food was so scarce.

------------------------------------------------

**Although there is no evidence to prove that Chikatilo even had an older brother, the story was ingrained on his memory from the time he was young and he went on to become one of Eastern Europe's most prolific and feared serial killers of all time.**

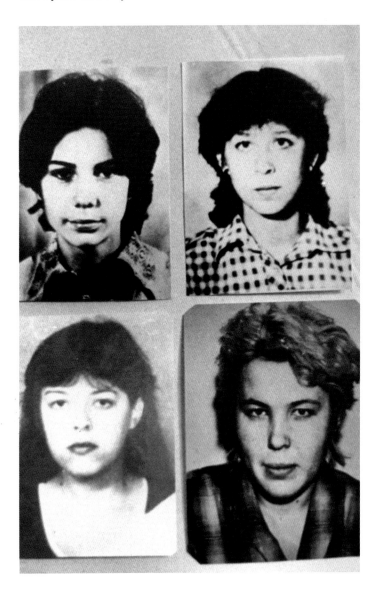

Despite suffering from impotency, Chikatilo married and fathered two children. He was a teacher at boys's school and described as a studious mentor and humble man, but things changed for Chikatilo in March 1981, when he was accused of the molestation of children in his care.

He moved his family to Shakhty to escape the slur on his reputation but soon discovered the sexual release that killing gave him. He bought a run-down shack where he lured children of both sexes and his first victim was a nine-year-old girl whom he intended to rape. However, when he was unable to perform sexually, he stabbed the girl to death in an uncontrolled rage and ejaculated.

It was to set the pattern for his series of killings, which involved women and young children. If girls were unavailable, he would target boys. The pattern of his crimes soon convinced police that they were looking for a serial killer.

Police dubbed him the "Rostov Ripper" and brought in a profiler to help in their quest to find the killer. The profile led to Chikatilo who eventually confessed to the murders of 56 people. Three bodies remained missing and the Rostov Ripper was eventually convicted of 53 killings and sentenced to death. He was executed by firing squad on 14th February 1994.

*LEFT: Portraits of four young female murder victims of Andrei Chikatilo*

*OPPOSITE: Full-length portraits of serial killer Andrei Chikatilo*

# Dennis Nilsen

Dennis Nilsen's troubled childhood was further deepened by a growing awareness of his latent homosexuality – erotic adolescent desires he sought to suppress.

- - - - - - - - - - - - - - - - - - - - - - - - - - - - - - - - - - - - - - - - - -

**At the age of 16, he enlisted in the British Army Catering Corps where he learned butchery skills and, having completed 11 years of military service, he discharged himself in 1972 and moved to London. Nilsen served as a constable in the Metropolitan Police for eight months, where he became morbidly fascinated with corpses in the morgue. Resigning from the Met, he commenced work as a Job Centre civil servant in 1974.**

Between 1978 and 1983, Dennis Andrew Nilsen – born in Fraserbourgh, Scotland, on 23rd November 1945 – lured 15 young men from the streets and pubs of north London back to his flat with promises of food, friendship and a place to stay, but took full advantage of the teeming anonymity of metropolitan London. He tended to prey upon young, vulnerable homosexual or homeless men – people who existed on the margins of society, people unlikely to be missed. He plied them with alcohol then, when they were no longer able to defend themselves, strangled them to death. Nilsen slept with the dead bodies of his victims, talking to them and having sex with them before storing them under the floorboards, sometimes for many months.

When the stench became unbearable and the flies breeding in the rotting corpses were overwhelming the flat, Nilsen would strip naked and dismember them on his flagstone kitchen floor, employing butchery skills he had learnt as a cook in the Army Catering Corps. He would then burn the remains in his back garden – topping the bonfire with a motor tyre to mask the stench of human flesh from his neighbours. It's believed that 12 men were murdered, violated and incinerated at Nilsen's Cricklewood address.

In 1982, Nilsen tried to quell his impulses by moving to a flat in Muswell Hill which had neither garden nor floorboards. However hard he tried though, Nilsen was unable to stop killing. He murdered three more men and stored their remains in bin bags which he hid in wardrobes and cupboards. Reacting to neighbours's complaints about the smell, he rendered down the remains in pots on his kitchen stove before flushing the grisly "stew" down the toilet. Eventually the drains blocked, and employees of a drain-cleaning firm discovered a suspicious organic deposit obstructing the pipework. Forensic analysis confirmed that the drains were blocked by human remains.

Having earned the nicknames the "Muswell Hill Murderer" and the "Kindly Killer", Nilsen was arrested and convicted on six counts of murder, and two of attempted murder at the Old Bailey on 24th October 1983. He was sentenced to life imprisonment with a minimum term to be served of 25 years. The Home Secretary

*ABOVE: Three men were murdered at Dennis Nilsen's home at 23 Cranley Gardens in Muswell Hill, London between 1981 and 1983*

*OPPOSITE: Serial killer Dennis Nilsen leaves Highgate Magistrate's Court in London with a police escort in February 1983*

subsequently imposed a whole life tariff meaning that Nilsen could never be released. On 13th July 2013, the European Court of Human Rights ruled that the whole life tariff without the possibility of release was illegal, but Nilsen continues to serve his sentence at the maximum security HMP Full Sutton in Yorkshire.

# Peter Sutcliffe

Peter William Sutcliffe was known as a solitary individual and left school at the age of 15 to pursue a series of basic employment opportunities, which included grave digging.

**After marrying in 1964, his wife experienced an unfortunate number of miscarriages and was later informed that she would never be able to have children. While many of Peter Sutcliffe's victims were prostitutes, some were not, and none of the women he attacked, or those he killed should have ever have been subjected to the horror of his heinous crimes.**

In 1969, Sutcliffe – born on 2nd June 1946 in Bingley, Yorkshire – carried out his first assault on a prostitute. He struck the woman over the head with a stone that he had placed in a sock. However, before he could continue the assault, he was distracted by the sound of a vehicle passing by and fled the scene. On 30th October 1975, 28-year-old Wilma McCann (a mother of four) became Sutcliffe's first murder victim. After being struck twice in the head with a hammer, she was violently stabbed 15 times in the neck, chest and abdomen. One of McCann's daughters committed suicide in 2007 as a result of decades of suffering and emotional turmoil following her mother's murder.

On 1st September 1979, the "Yorkshire Ripper", as he had been dubbed, murdered 20-year-old Barbara Leach, a Bradford University student. Before he hid Leach's body beneath a pile of bricks near the university grounds, he mutilated the young woman. This was his 16th attack, and it caused uproar within the press due to the fact that the young victim had been a university undergraduate. Women across Bradford and the surrounding areas became scared to go out alone.

The Yorkshire Ripper's method of attack, assault and murder included bludgeoning his victim's head with a hammer then slicing up their body up with a knife or sharpened screwdriver. Several of the victims had also been sexually assaulted, which was established by traces of

semen found in their underwear. Eventually, it was known that Sutcliffe wore a V-neck sweater on his legs underneath his trousers, with the V-neck exposing his genitals and the padded elbow patches giving his knees protection, so that he could hold down and mutilate his victims.

It was not until 1981 that Sutcliffe was to be identified and detained. On 2nd January, police stopped Sutcliffe when they spotted false number plates on the vehicle he was driving. While under police interview, he was questioned in relation to the Yorkshire Ripper case as he matched the physical descriptions given by survivors of the horrific attacks. After two long days of exhaustive questioning, Sutcliffe confessed that he was the Yorkshire Ripper and provided police with details of how he had murdered his victims. He claimed that he was following the voice of God who had instructed him to brutally end the lives of the women he attacked.

At his trial, he pleaded guilty to seven counts of attempted murder and was convicted of murdering 13 women. Sutcliffe was dealt a sentence of life imprisonment and later moved to Broadmoor Hospital with suspected mental health issues. Sutcliffe continues to carry out his sentence today.

In February 2017, Peter Sutcliffe was involved in a bust-up with child killer, Ian Huntley. Both men are serving time at HMP Frankland in County Durham.

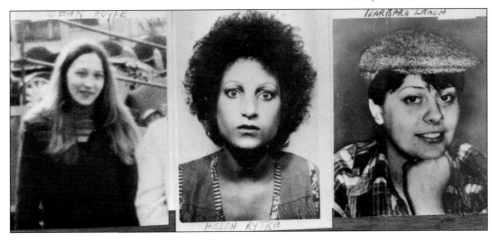

*LEFT: Three of the young women murdered by Peter Sutcliffe – left to right; Jean Royle, Helga Rytka and Barbara Leach*

*OPPOSITE: Peter Sutcliffe in police custody, 1983*

# Clifford Olson

Christine Weller's death was the first in a series of murders by Clifford Olson, born in 1940, that would claim the lives of at least 10 more child victims between the ages of 9 and 18 in the Greater Vancouver area.

- - - - - - - - - - - - - - - - - - - - - - - - - - - - - - - - - - - - - - - - - - - - -

**There was nothing to suggest that Olson, who grew up in a "normal family", would turn into a child predator and monster. There had been no childhood traumas, but he began to find himself constantly in trouble with the police, much to the embarrassment of his family, particularly his parents. They long gave up hope of changing their son's behaviour, but they did try to help him when they could. By 1980, Olson had only spent four years of his adult life outside of prison.**

Christine Weller, 12, was late home for dinner at 5.00pm on 17th November 1980. She had met with some friends after school and borrowed a classmate's bike in order to cycle the three-minute ride to her home at the Bonanza Motel in Surrey, British Columbia, just 15 miles from Vancouver. Christine was a tomboy who enjoyed being out, especially with her friends, so when she didn't return home, her parents assumed she was staying with someone she knew, as she had on a few occasions before. It took them nearly a week to file a missing person's report and to make matters worse police treated Christine as a runaway. However, when police found the young girl's borrowed bike just a few streets away from her home, they knew that something was wrong. On 25th December, her decomposing body was found by a dog walker at the back of a dump in Richmond where it was discovered she had multiple stab wounds to her chest and abdomen and had been strangled with a belt.

Following the frenzied attack and murder of Christine, Olson's second victim was abducted in April 1981. Colleen Daignault, 13, was found five months later, while Daryn Johnsrude, 16, was kidnapped and killed the same month. At least nine more victims disappeared during the months throughout 1981, including nine-year-old Simon Partington, who was brutally sexually assaulted and raped before being strangled by Olson.

Criminal profiling was extremely different in the early 1980s and what confused police for a time was the fact that Olson's victims included both girls and boys from various age groups. Little was understood about sex offenders at the time and the case of Daryn was not linked to the two earlier murders of Christine and Colleen until much later. He used the "gift of the gab" and verbal traps to lure youngsters to secluded locations or into motel rooms. Here, Olson's victims were plied with alcohol and drugs, rendering them helpless before he raped them and often murdered them. However, some of his victims, he did let go and one anonymous victim revealed how he enticed kids with promises of money for landscaping work. He would gain the trust of some of his younger "employees" and groomed them with gifts and

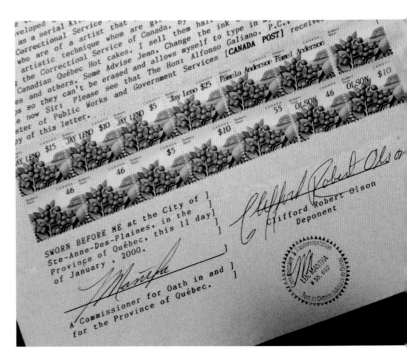

*ABOVE: Clifford Olson 'designed' a series of postage stamps while in prison (some honouring Jay Leno and some honouring himself)*

money, before reverting into a sexual predator. It was never firmly established why Olson killed some victims and not others – he didn't even seem to know himself. What he did say following his arrest, in the third person was: "...children: young boys and girls are frequently desirable victims by the serial killer for sex...".

Olson died in prison from cancer in 2011.

# Pedro Lopez

The seventh of 13 children, born to a prostitute in Colombia in 1949, Pedro Lopez faced hardship and difficulties at home, but anything was better than life on the streets.

- - - - - - - - - - - - - - - - - - - - - - - - - - - - - - - - - - - - - - - - - - - - - - -

**When his overbearing mother found him at the age of eight touching the chest of his younger sister in an inappropriate way, he was literally thrown out, into his worst nightmare, in a city where crime was 50% higher than any other in the world. When a man offered him a place to stay and food to eat, Lopez thought he was safe. He couldn't have been more wrong.**

The man eventually let Lopez escape the stench of the abandoned building where he had taken him and sodomised him repeatedly, but for the following year he remained alone and afraid. He slept in doorways and alleyways, avoiding anyone he could, only venturing out at night to search for food amongst the city's bins and rubbish tips. However, after 12 months, he began to travel and it was the start of a journey that would turn Lopez into a sexual predator, a horrific rapist and murderer of more than 350 children across South America. Later known as "The Monster of the Andes", Lopez was eventually taken in as a child by a couple, horrified by his plight, living in Bogota who sent him to a school for orphans. At the age of 12, he was sexually molested by a male teacher, so he stole some money from the school office and ran away from what had been a safe haven for the past few years. He returned to the streets of his native Colombia where, with no skills and no formal education, he had little choice but to beg for food for the next six years. He began stealing cars in order to survive and was sent to prison where, after just two days, at the age of 18, he was brutally gang-raped by inmates. What little sanity he had by this time had long gone and he murdered three of the four men that raped him with a makeshift knife. He vowed that no one would ever touch him again.

He blamed his mother for his troubles and had difficulty relating to women on any level, particularly sexually. He fled to Peru following his release from prison where he began stalking and killing girls from local Indian tribes. The attempted abduction of a nine-year-old girl from one tribe saw Lopez tortured and threatened with being buried alive by the Ayachuchos in northern Peru, but he was saved from certain death by an American missionary who handed him over to the authorities. He was deported to Ecuador but it is thought he had already killed more than 100 little girls by this time. The authorities noticed a rise in missing children, but put the disappearances down to the fast-growing sex slave rings in South America. However, a flash flood in 1980 near Ambato in Ecuador caused a rethink when the bodies of four missing children were uncovered. A few days later, 12-year-old Marie Poveda was snatched as she shopped with her mother at a market. Carvina Proveda's cries for help to stop the man abducting her daughter brought a rapid response from stall owners who brought Lopez to the ground and held him until police arrived. His ramblings caused them to think they were dealing with a madman. He eventually confessed to

kidnapping his victims and raping them. He always carried out the rapes and killings by strangulation in daylight so that he could stare into their eyes, feeling pleasure and sexual excitement as their lives faded in front of him. Sometimes, he would act out tea parties with the dead children by propping them up, even in their makeshift graves and talking to them.

He was sentenced to life in prison in Ecuador, but in the middle of the night in the summer of 1998, he was released on the Colombian border. No one knows his whereabouts.

*ABOVE: Pedro Lopez*

# David Berkowitz

The summer of 1976 saw New York City terrorised by a lone gunman with a .44 calibre Bulldog revolver.

- - - - - - - - - - - - - - - - - - - - - - - - - - - - - - - - - - - - - - - - - - - - -

**In little over a year, six victims were dead and seven others injured. The huge manhunt saw David Berkowitz – also known as the "Son of Sam" – evade police at every turn.**

Adopted as a baby, with a troubled childhood, Berkowitz became known to neighbours as spoilt and difficult. He was discharged from the army in 1974 and suffered an identity crisis upon discovering that he was adopted and illegitimate. After his arrest in August 1977, Berkowitz claimed he was suffering from demonic possession and later declared he was a member of a murderous Satanic cult.

The shootings began in the Bronx on 29th July when friends Donna Lauria (18) and Jody Valenti (19) were shot in a car around 1.00am. Donna was killed instantly, but Jody survived. Queens became the scene of the next attack in October when Carl Denaro (25) and Rosemary Keenan (38) were shot at. The glass of the vehicle suddenly shattered and Keenan drove off in panic. Neither of them realised it

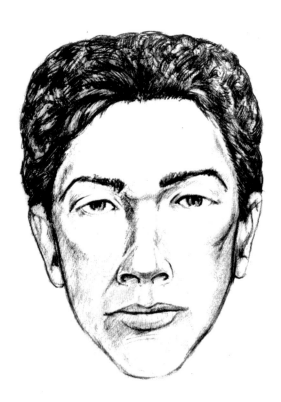

LEFT and ABOVE: David Berkowitz's mug shot and a police sketch based on descriptions by witnesses to shootings of Stacy Moskowitz and Robert Violante

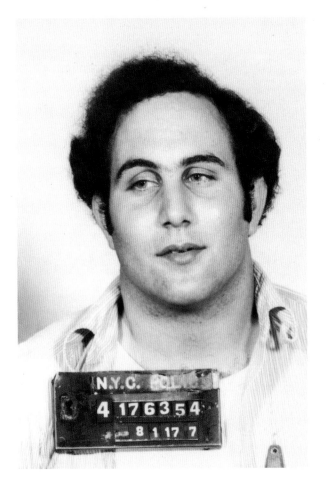

was a shooting, despite the fact that Carl Denaro was shot in the head. At first, police did not link the two attacks, partly because the crimes were investigated in different boroughs.

The following month, Donna DeMasi and Joanne Lomino were chatting after a night out. They were approached and shot. Donna was hit in the neck, but Joanne was shot in the back and left paraplegic. On 30th January 1977, engaged couple John Diel and Christine Freund were shot as they sat in a car. In a panic, John drove from the scene, but Christine had been shot twice and later died in hospital. From this point on, the police were fairly sure that the shootings were connected and that the perpetrator was targeting young women with

ABOVE: *The scene where the last of Berkowitz's victims were shot at Shore Parkway and Bay 16th St*

long dark hair. Virginia Voskerichian, 19, was killed on her way home from college when she was shot in the head, despite trying to defend herself with her school books. It was 8th March 1977 and this murder was different. The young woman had been alone rather than with another person, and the time was early evening rather than late at night or during the early hours.

The task force, charged with capturing the killer, was Operation Omega led by D. I. Timothy J Dowd, but just over a month later in April, two more young victims, Alexander Esau and Valentina Suriani, were both shot dead. Close to their bodies, police found a letter from the "Son of Sam" full of misspelt words claiming he would carry on his "work".

Further shootings followed, but Berkowitz was witnessed receiving a parking ticket close to one crime scene. The information was passed to police who arrested him on 10th August. He confessed to the killings, but during his trial was heard to chant that Stacy (Moskowitz), one of his later victims, was a whore. He was sentenced to 25 years to life for each of the murders, to be served consecutively.

# Dennis Rader

When Dennis Rader joined the US Air Force at the age of 21 in 1966, he continued the unremarkable pattern that had been his life.

**However, he began paying for sex when his penchant for bondage activities were rejected by the women he had "relationships" with. He turned to stalking a number of victims, but took things no further despite his fascination with wondering what it would be like to strangle someone to death.**

He married a local woman from his hometown of Wichita in 1971 and two years later began night school at the State University. This gave him unprecedented access to a large number of women. Losing his job at the same time meant deep depression and a growing restlessness that would ultimately lead to murder.

He began stalking the women close to where his wife worked in 1974 and dreamt of binding, torturing and killing his victims. Known as the "BTK" killer after his own obsession with Bind, Torture, Kill, his focus turned to Julie Otero, 34, and her 11-year-old daughter, Josephine. Rader was particularly drawn to the woman, whom he admired for her beauty. He put together a kit consisting of a gun, knives, cord and tools for breaking and entering while he observed the daily comings and goings of the Otero family.

On 15th January 1974, Rader broke into their home sometime after 8.00am and motioned for the family to go upstairs at gunpoint. He told them that he was a "wanted" criminal who needed money and a car. The family was tied up and 38-year-old Joe Otero had a plastic bag placed over his head. He fought hard, but Rader used a cord ligature and the bag to kill him before attempting to strangle Julie Otero with his bare hands. It seemed to take forever for the woman to die and she revived after a time before Rader strangled her again and killed her. He then took nine-year-old Joey Otero into his bedroom and strangled and suffocated the child who died lying face down on the floor. Rader later told police that he had taken a chair into the room to watch the boy die. Josephine was taken to the basement and hung after Radar failed to strangle her in her own bedroom. How terrified this child must have been is almost impossible to comprehend. The victims were found by the three older Otero children who had already left for school the day Rader broke into their home.

His next victim was 21-year-old Kathryn Bright. She was stalked and watched by Rader until her untimely death in April 1974. He broke into her home and waited. Kathryn arrived home on 4th April with her brother, Kevin, 19, to be confronted by Rader brandishing a gun. He tied up both victims, but Kevin managed to get loose and suffered two gun shot wounds in a vicious fight with the killer. While Kevin lay apparently dead, Rader first strangled Kathryn before butchering her with a knife. Meanwhile, Kevin – who had just been stunned by a gunshot wound to his head – managed to flee the apartment and raise the alarm. Rader was forced to make a quick exit.

In October that year, Rader sent a letter to the editor of the "Wichita Eagle" anonymously claiming responsibility for the crimes. The letter directed the editor to search for another letter in the Wichita Public Library, but the police picked it up to find Rader using his chosen code for the first time – "Bind them, Torture them, Kill them, BTK".

His next murder came in 1977 and the killing continued until 1991, some 14 years before his arrest in 2005. His next five victims were all women who he strangled, either with a belt, his hands or a pair of tights or stockings. It was his taunting letters to the police and various newspapers that would be his downfall. He is currently serving 10 consecutive life sentences in Kansas.

*LEFT: A mask used in one of the crimes is displayed during Dennis Rader's sentencing hearing in August 2005*

*OPPOSITE: Dennis Rader in court on the first day of his sentencing at the Sedgwick County Courthouse*

# Ted Bundy

Ted Bundy stated in his final interview, before he faced execution for the rape and murder of more than 30 women and girls, that one of the driving forces for all serial killers, in his opinion, is pornography.

- - - - - - - - - - - - - - - - - - - - - - - - - - - - - - - - - - - - - - - - - - - - - - - -

**Talking from Florida State Prison in January 1989, following 10 years of incarceration, he described how pornography is a serious addiction.**

Bundy was arrested on 15th February 1978 in Florida. It is believed that the number of women and girls he actually killed is close to 50 or more. He was convicted on 31st July 1979 and sentenced to death.

Bundy had grown up in a loving, caring family where he and his siblings had been the focus for his parents, although he later discovered that his "parents" were his maternal grandparents and that his older sister, Louise, was in fact his mother. He said that he had never been mistreated and his childhood was happy and content. He was eventually adopted by his mother's husband, Johnny Bundy. The changes that came about in this "all American boy", in his words, were gradual – and it started with pornography which, over time, turned into an obsession and an addiction. This led to needing more than violent pornography and the deaths of many innocent women and girls while Bundy searched for that ever-increasing need for more excitement.

For Bundy, pornography could only go so far and he reached a "jumping off point", where he needed to act out his fantasies.

Even an FBI study into serial homicides points to the most common habits for these perpetrators being violent pornography. At the end of the 1980s and into the 1990s, hardcore pornography was being cited as one of the devastating links to violent sexual behaviour.

Bundy was initially arrested in Utah in 1975 for aggravated kidnapping, but it became increasingly clear that he was probably responsible for a large number of crimes, including sexual assault and murder. After being incarcerated, he made two dramatic escapes, committed three murders and many other assaults before he was finally captured for good in 1978. By this time, he was already facing murder charges in Colorado and was suspected of committing a number of other murders across other American states.

Handsome and charismatic, Bundy found his victims easily. Although approaching his execution he described some of his crimes in detail, Bundy never divulged his earlier killing experiences and there is no record of when he actually began his crimes. It is strongly suspected that he began killing women during the early 1970s while studying law at the University of Utah, but some authority figures believe he began killing much earlier while still a teenager.

His 1968 Volkswagen Beetle was the scene of many of his crimes, and he became a prolific kidnapper, rapist, serial killer and necrophiliac, who would often revisit his victims and commit sexual acts until wild animals or putrefaction made further assaults impossible.

Just one day after his final interview, on 24th January 1989, Bundy was executed in the electric chair.

*LEFT: The sign at the Naked Lady Saloon celebrates the execution of serial killer Ted Bundy*

*OPPOSITE: Ted Bundy acts up in courtroom after the judge has departed*

# John Wayne Gacy

In Chicago, Illinois, between 1972 and 1978, at least 33 teenage boys and young men became victims of John Wayne Gacy, the American rapist and serial killer.

**Gacy, born in 1942, was known for his charitable work as "Pogo the Clown", which saw him nicknamed as "Killer Clown" once his dark secrets were revealed.**

Gacy endured a difficult relationship with his abusive father and was regularly beaten with a belt, while, at the age of nine, he was molested by a family friend. Although he married, Gacy had a number of homosexual experiences, but also managed to climb the social ladder and became the outstanding vice-president of the Waterloo Jaycees in Illinois. The year was 1967 and Gacy was working for his father-in-law as the manager of three Kentucky Fried Chicken restaurants. He worked tirelessly. He also fathered two children. His first sexual assault on a teenage boy happened in August 1967.

Jaycee life in Waterloo was not all about "doing good" – wife swapping, drugs and prostitution were rife. Gacy was not afraid to try any of them and was regularly unfaithful to his wife. Pornography was a big part of Jaycee life too and Gacy lured fellow Jaycee's son, Donald Voorhees, 15, with the promise of watching pornographic films. Gacy gave Donald copious amounts of alcohol and persuaded the youth to perform oral sex on him.

More teenagers followed, many of whom believed that Gacy had been commissioned to conduct homosexual research. Each was paid $50. Donald eventually told his father about Gacy's sexual assault and he was indicted on charges of sodomy in May 1968. On leaving prison in 1970, Gacy went to live with his mother in Chicago. Less than a year later, he was charged with another sexual assault, but the case was dropped when the boy failed to show in court. Gacy then bought a house in the Norwood Park Township. He remarried and his wife and stepdaughters moved in to his house in Summerdale Avenue.

His social status was also beginning to rise again amongst the local community, but there lurked a dark side to Gacy. He started his own construction company and raped a young man, whom he employed, while away on a business trip. Gacy then murdered Timothy Jack McCoy, 15, in January 1972. He ended up stabbing the youth repeatedly and ejaculated while murdering the boy.

It was then that Gacy realised that death was the "ultimate thrill". McCoy was the only victim Gacy stabbed. All others were killed by asphyxiation, strangulation and tourniquet. Many of these teenage boys and young men were buried underneath Gacy's home.

On 22nd December 1978, after human remains were found by police, Gacy confessed to the murders and was tried in Cook County for 33 murders. He was found guilty and executed by lethal injection in May 1994.

*ABOVE: Following intensive research, investigation and surveillance, John Wayne Gacy was arrested by the Des Plaines Police Department in December 1978*

*ABOVE: Police use a ground-penetrating radar device behind an apartment building on Chicago's Northwest Side in search of as many as four more possible victims of murderer John Wayne Gacy*

# Rodney Alcala

Responsible for the murders of four women and a 12-year-old girl in Southern California between 1977 and 1979, Rodney Alcala, was sentenced to death in 2010.

- - - - - - - - - - - - - - - - - - - - - - - - - - - - - - - - - - - - - - - - - - - - - - - - - - - - - - - - - - - -

**Born in 1943, the convicted rapist and serial killer was also given a further 25 years to life in 2013 for pleading guilty to two murders in New York in 1971 and 1977. Alcala may be responsible for many other killings and, while conservative estimates moot 50 murders, others believe that the number of victims he killed may run into the hundreds.**

At the age of 12, Alcala moved with his family to Los Angeles and, five years later, joined the Army. He was discharged on medical grounds in 1964 and diagnosed as having antisocial personality disorder. Four years later, Alcala lured eight-year-old Tali Shapiro into his Los Angeles apartment where she was raped and beaten before he evaded police. His first victim survived her attack, but his second victim was found raped and strangled in her New York apartment. The murder of 23-year-old flight attendant, Cornelia Michel Crilley, would remain unsolved for the next 40 years.

Using the alias John Burger, Alcala – by now a UCLA Fine Arts graduate – obtained a summer job at a New Hampshire children's art camp, where his FBI "wanted" poster was spotted by two vigilant youngsters attending the course. Upon his arrest, he was transported back to California, but Tali's parents refused to allow their daughter to testify in his case, and he was paroled after just 17 months in prison for assault. On his release, he assaulted a 13-year-old girl and was sent back to prison where he served 24 months. It is believed that he killed 23-year-old Ellen Jane Hover when his parole officer allowed him

to travel to New York after his second release from prison in 1977. In 1979, he was sentenced to death for the murder of 12-year-old Robin Samsoe, in California, but the sentence was overturned when it transpired that jurors had been informed of his previous sex offences.

In 2003, Alcala's DNA was linked to four murder cases and, in 2006, the murder of Robin Samsoe was tied into the official investigation. In 2010, he was convicted and sentenced to death for the murders of Robin Samsoe, Jill Parenteau, Charlotte Lamb, Georgia Wixted and Jill Barcomb. All the victims's bodies were found posed in a specific and careful way. Having worked as a photographer, Alcala had lured many women and children, including teenage boys, to pose for him. A number of his photographs featured naked children. In 2010, 120 of these images were publicly released in order that the "sitters" might be identified. It is believed that many of these victims could have been murdered at Alcala's hands – while more than 900 of the photographs were too sexually explicit to be released.

In 2016, Alcala was charged with the murder of a woman identified as one of his photo subjects.

*LEFT: Convicted California serial killer Rodney Alcala is pictured in Manhattan Supreme Court in New York in January 2013*

*OPPOSITE: Leon Borstein with photo of his girlfriend Cornelia Crilley, who was murdered by Rodney Alcala*

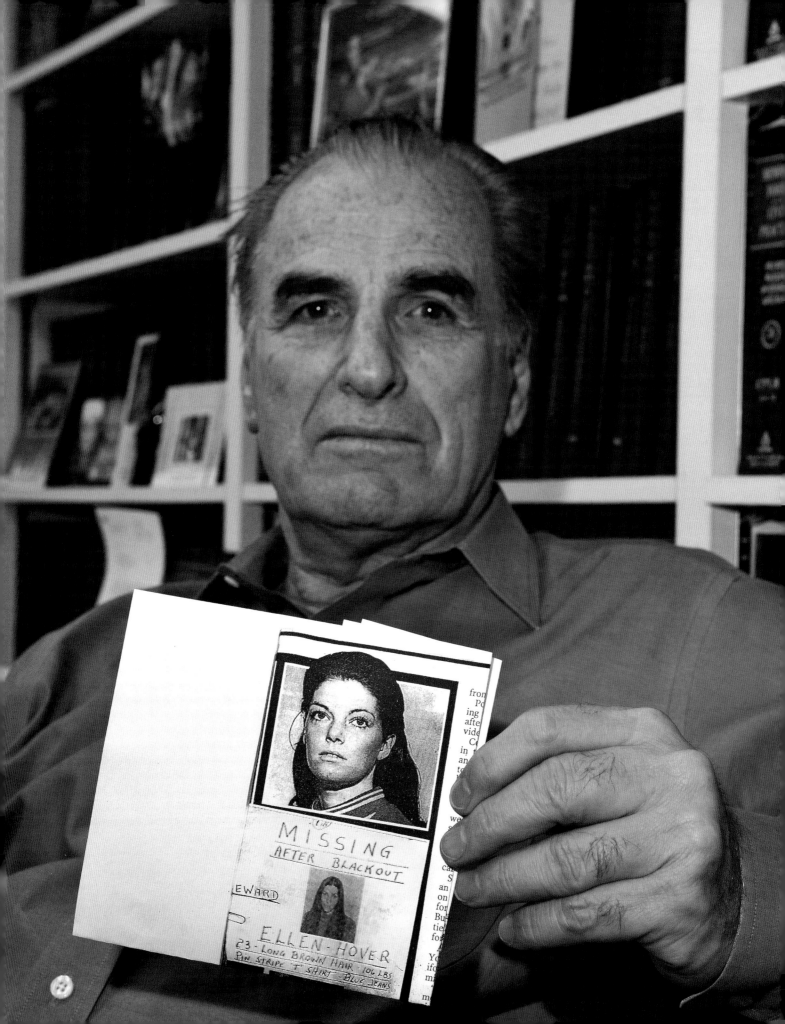

MISSING
AFTER BLACKOUT

EWARD

ELLEN HOVER
23 - LONG BROWN HAIR - 106 LBS
PIN STRIPE T SHIRT - BLUE JEANS

from
Po
ing
afte
vide
Co
in t
an
t

we

ca
S
an
on
for
Bu
tie
for

A
Yo
if
m

# Patrick Mackay

At 15, Patrick Mackay was diagnosed as a psychopath likely to kill. He was placed in the care of the Moss Side Hospital, Liverpool, in 1968 where he remained as an in-patient until he was released in 1972.

- - - - - - - - - - - - - - - - - - - - - - - - - - - - - - - - - - - - - - - - - - - - - - - -

**Mackay was born in Middlesex in 1952, the son of a violent alcoholic father although, at 10 years old, he was unable to accept his father's death, telling people that he was still alive.**

Mackay developed into a deeply disturbed teenager. He erupted into fits of extreme anger and had violent tantrums. He bullied children, mugged passers-by and stole from the homes of the elderly. He then began to develop a murderous side to his personality; he attempted to kill his mother and his aunt by strangulation and nearly succeeded in killing a younger boy. He also indulged in arson by attempting to burn down a church.

The maturing Mackay developed an obsession with the Nazis. Embracing his own Nazi theme, he reinvented himself as the world dictator "Franklin Bollvolt The First". He dressed in a storm-trooper's uniform and demanded that people use his Bollvolt name when they addressed him; he considered it: "... a name to be feared and remembered. Like Hitler's".

When Mackay wasn't indulging in Nazi fantasies, he was drinking heavily and taking drugs. In 1973, Mackay was befriended by a Catholic priest, Father Anthony Crean. Mackay abused Crean's friendship and trust by breaking into his home and stealing money. He was arrested and prosecuted for the theft, and ordered to reimburse Crean, but his prosecution for the theft caused a fatal rift to fester with the priest.

In 1974, Mackay was living with friends in north London. When he declared himself to be possessed by demons, his alarmed friends threw him out of the house. He later returned to rob them and received a six-month sentence for burglary. In March 1975, Mackay killed Father Crean with an axe. He split the priest's skull open, exposing the brain, and then watched as his former friend slowly bled to death before stabbing Crean's corpse repeatedly to make sure he really was dead.

The police, aware of Mackay's recent history with Crean, arrested him as their prime murder suspect. Detectives also suspected that Mackay might be linked to at least 12 other killings of elderly people, victims who had been stabbed or strangled during robberies. After his arrest, the ever-arrogant "Nazi" took delight in bragging that he had murdered 11 people. He was reported to have thrown a young female au pair from a train at New Cross, stabbed victims in their own homes, bludgeoned them with lead pipes, and hurled a vagrant off a bridge.

Police charged Mackay with five murders. However, owing to a lack of evidence, two of these charges were dropped. He was tried and convicted of manslaughter (due to diminished responsibility) in November 1975. Patrick Mackay remains incarcerated, having received a sentence of life imprisonment.

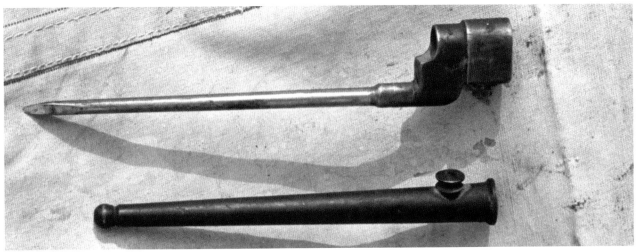

*ABOVE: A bayonet belonging to Mackay thought to have been used as a murder weapon*

*OPPOSITE: Patrick Mackay*

# Donald Neilson

From being bullied at school and during his National Service, Donald Neilson became notorious as "The Black Panther".

In 1965, to supplement his meagre earnings, Donald Neilson – born in Bradford in 1936 – took up house burglary, then armed post office robberies. Three sub-postmasters who resisted were shot dead. When he was "working" Nielson disguised his appearance by wearing a dark balaclava. He was also described by policemen as "having fought like a cornered animal" as they tried to catch him and this led to the press dubbing him "The Black Panther".

In 1975, Neilson kidnapped 17-year-old schoolgirl Lesley Whittle, the heiress of a major coach travel business. She was abducted from her bedroom and bound with sticking plaster while her family slept before being carried to the kidnapper's car. He left a ransom note demanding £50,000, giving instructions how the money was to be dropped by Lesley's brother Ronald. He warned the family not to inform the police. Lesley was left bound and gagged, with a wire noose around her neck, on a narrow shelf above a chasm in a 54-foot drainage shaft attached to disused mines in Bathpool Park, Kidsgrove, in Staffordshire.

The Whittle family ignored Neilson's warning and the local police brought in Scotland Yard. The involvement of competing police forces led to a shambolic breakdown in communication and a leak of information to the press.

Three attempts at delivering the ransom were bungled and Lesley's emaciated body was eventually discovered, suspended from the noose in the drainage shaft. It was never ascertained whether an enraged Neilson had deliberately pushed Lesley off the shelf of rock, or if Lesley fell to her death accidentally.

On the same night as the final failed ransom drop, Neilson, as "The Black Panther", held up a railway goods depot and a security guard was fatally wounded. The police linked this robbery and the post office raids to "The Black Panther" and, a week later, Neilson's getaway car was identified near the goods depot. In the car was a copy of Lesley Whittle's ransom instruction tape. This confirmed that "The Black Panther" and the Whittle kidnapper were one and the same person.

In December 1975, Neilson, who had returned to robbing sub-post offices, was – following a dramatic, failed gunpoint abduction of two police officers in their patrol car – overpowered by the officers, with the assistance of customers queuing at the Junction Chip Shop, in Rainworth, Nottinghamshire. The police had decided to pick up the man who had been acting suspiciously as they drove around the area.

Neilson was arrested while in possession of two of his trademark panther hoods. He was taken to Kidsgrove police station to be interviewed where he confessed to the kidnap of Lesley Whittle, and to his "Panther" raids in an 18-page statement.

Donald Neilson was tried at Oxford Crown Court on 14th June 1976. He was charged with four murders, one count of attempted murder, grievous bodily harm, robbery, kidnap and firearms offences. He was convicted on 1st July 1976, and received five life sentences with no possibility of parole. Suffering from motor neurone disease and pneumonia, Neilson died in Norwich Prison on 18th December 2011.

*OPPOSITE: A police mugshot of Donald Neilson*

*ABOVE: Mourners at the funeral of Lesley Whittle, including her mother Dorothy who is supported between her son Ronald and her sister Sandra Dorrell*

# Charles Sobhraj

Charles Sobhraj felt neglected once his mother and her boyfriend had children of their own and began to commit petty crimes. Burglary featured heavily in his subsequent years and he was sentenced to imprisonment on several occasions before he eventually turned to murder.

- - - - - - - - - - - - - - - - - - - - - - - - - - - - - - - - - - - - - - - - - - -

**Bharat Rajpurohit, better known as Charles Sobhraj, was born on 6<sup>th</sup> April 1944. His Indian Sindhi father abandoned his Vietnamese mother while Sobhraj was a child and his mother started a relationship with a French army lieutenant.**

After his second stint in prison, Sobhraj married Chantal Compagnon and the pair travelled through Eastern Europe using fake documents while robbing tourists of their money. Arriving in Mumbai in 1970, Sobhraj ran a car theft and smuggling operation and was later arrested for an attempted armed robbery on a jewellery store. Following this, Sobhraj and his wife spent the next two years on the run, travelling through various countries in Eastern Europe and the Middle East using stolen passports.

He became known as "The Serpent" due to his numerous escapes from jail and his ability to evade the authorities almost everywhere he went.

Sobhraj's murders were varied in their execution and demonstrated paranoia as the only probable motive within most of the cases. His first murder victim, Teresa Knowlton, was found drowned in a tidal pool after she had threatened to expose Sobhraj and his significant other for their crimes. Later, two Dutch students met Sobhraj in Hong Kong and were invited back to Thailand, where the killer poisoned the couple and then nursed them back to health as a means of getting

them to help in his evil plans. After a brief scare of being exposed, Sobhraj strangled the two students and burned their bodies, which were discovered on 16<sup>th</sup> December 1975.

Sobhraj continued to target tourists and travelled between Nepal, Calcutta, Singapore and India using the stolen passports of some of his earlier victims. He closely avoided capture after three French companions (who he had met through fraudulent activities at an earlier time) suspected him of serial killing and reported him to the Thai authorities. Although he was arrested and questioned, he avoided conviction, as the Thai authorities feared that such a murder trial would have a large and negative impact on the country's tourist industry.

In July 1976, Sobhraj was finally captured after being overpowered by some French students that he had attempted to drug. After his arrest, Sobhraj was sent to Tihar Prison. His time inside consisted of bribing prison guards with gems that he had hidden within his body and the hiring and firing of many lawyers in order to gain media attention.

Sobhraj is unlike many other serial killers. His motives for killing were not linked to deeply-rooted violent impulses or mental disorders. He had become a "celebrity" and enjoyed the attention he attracted from the media, often charging large sums of money for interviews and film rights.

Following his release from prison, he returned to France where he was arrested and is currently serving a life sentence as issued in Nepal for the murder of a US citizen and for fraudulent activities. He is a wanted criminal in other countries and will likely serve the rest of his life on trial and behind bars.

*LEFT: Charles Sobhraj gets down from a police vehicle with his face covered by a handkerchief as a crowd of media representatives swarm around him outside the District Court in Kathmandu, September 2003*

# Dean Corll

Dean Corll revelled in giving away free sweets to children – earning himself the nickname "The Candy Man".

**While serving as a soldier, Corll discovered he was homosexual and in 1965 he was honourably discharged from the military allowing him to return to Houston and assist his mother in running her growing confectionery enterprise.**

Dean Corll (born in Fort Wayne, Indiana, in 1939) preferred the company of young teenage boys – two in particular; Elmer Wayne Henley, aged 14, and David Brooks, aged 15. The unlikely trio were often observed driving around Houston in Corll's van but curious comments and gossip turned to horror when Henley shot Corll to death in his own home. Police officers questioned Henley at length while an almost unbelievable tale of brutal torture, sodomy and murder came to light.

Henley told officers that Corll had paid him and David Brooks $200 for each boy they lured to Corll's house with promises of free drink and drugs. Once the boys were inside the house, they were then at the mercy of Corll who seized them and subjected them to brutal torture and murder.

Officers discovered a torture chamber, with a "torture board" fitted with handcuffs, lengths of rope and a large dildo. The carpeted floor had been covered with plastic sheeting.

Henley spoke freely about what had occurred in Corll's house, and the part he had played in the torture and murder of his young friends. Corll had even forced the victims to write notes to their parents saying they were running away.

Henley took the police to Corll's burial grounds where forensic officers recovered 27 decomposing corpses. Post-mortem investigations revealed that some of them, aged between nine and 21 years, had been strangled to death, while others had been shot. All the corpses showed signs of torture – genitals had been chewed, pubic hairs ripped out, some victims had been castrated, items had been driven into the boys's rectums, and glass rods had been forced into their urethras. All had been raped anally and their mouths had been taped to stifle their screams.

Matters had come to a head when Henley brought his girlfriend and a male friend to Corll's house. The torturing killer had been enraged that Henley dared bring a girl into his house, but he calmed himself down and gave the youngsters alcohol and drugs. Inevitably, they all passed out. Henley awoke to find himself handcuffed to the "torture board" while the other two were bound with electrical tape.

*ABOVE: A newspaper headline tells the gruesome details of the sex related murders of teenage boys committed by electrician Dean Corll, stands out from the lawn of Corll's home*

Henley, aware of what Corll was about to do to him, persuaded Corll to release him so he could help torture, rape and murder his friends. Henley, following Corll's instructions, attempted to rape his girlfriend, while the killer tried to rape the other boy. However, the boy fought back, frustrating his attacker, and in the confusion, Henley seized a gun and killed Corll, shooting him six times. Henley then called the police.

Elmer Henley and David Brooks were both tried for their crimes in what became known as "The Houston Mass Murders". Brooks received a life sentence. Henley received six life sentences for six murders, but his shooting of Corll was judged an act of self-defence.

# The Zodiac Killer

The Zodiac Killer was the name given to the unidentified murderer responsible for taking the lives of at least five victims between 1968 and 1969.

**Taunting letters and cryptograms were sent to the police department charged with investigating the case. The target victims consisted of both males and females aged between 16 and 29.**

His first victims were Betty Lou Jensen and David Faraday, two high school students on a first date on 20th December 1968. The couple were shot dead as they were getting out of their car. Jensen's body was found nearly 30 feet away from the vehicle with five shots in her back while Faraday was killed by a single close-range shot to the head.

Nearly seven months later, the Zodiac Killer targeted Darlene Ferrin and Michael Mageau while they were parked at Blue Rocks Springs Park on the night of 4th July 1969. Shortly after midnight, a brown car

– believed to be either a Ford Mustang or Chevrolet Corvair – pulled into the car park for several minutes before driving off. It returned less than five minutes later and the driver exited the car and approached Ferrin's vehicle shining a torch at her face. He raised a handgun and shot five 9mm rounds through the passenger window hitting Mageau in the face and chest, the bullets tearing through his body and hitting Ferrin. As she tried to turn away from the attacker, the Zodiac Killer fired at her with bullets penetrating her arms and torso. A local resident heard the shots and called the police who arrived along with an ambulance shortly after the killer's departure.

*ABOVE: San Francisco police circulated this composite of the Bay Area's Zodiac Killer*

*ABOVE: An undated copy of a cryptogram sent to "The San Francisco Chronicle" in November 1969 by the Zodiac Killer*

Ferrin's wounds were so severe that she died in the ambulance. Mageau was rushed straight into surgery and despite suffering gun shot wounds to the neck, jaw and knee survived the ordeal and was able to give a description of the attacker's characteristics. Forty-five minutes after the shooting, a man called the Vellejo Police Department claiming he was responsible for the attack at Blue Rocks Spring Park and for the murders of Jensen and Faraday more than six months before.

The Zodiac Killer murdered three further victims and continued to taunt the police with letters and greetings cards along with cryptograms; most of which were difficult to decipher. He threatened to target children on a school bus and claimed he was collecting slaves for the afterlife. His desire to become a celebrity was evident as he instructed for one of his ciphers to be printed on the front page of

"The San Francisco Chronicle" citing that he would go on a mass killing spree if the authorities and media failed to carry out his demand. In other communications, the Zodiac boasted of his kill count using his signature symbol followed by a number. In a letter, in 1974, he indicated that his final death tally had allegedly reached 37.

There have been several suspects with regard to the identity of the Zodiac Killer but, due to inconclusive evidence and DNA analysis, the murderer remains anonymous.

*BELOW: Deborah Perez claimed in April 2009 that her father Guy Ward Hendrickson (who died in 1983 of cancer) was the Zodiac Killer*

# Wayne Boden

Between 1969 and 1971 Wayne Boden became a notorious serial killer obsessed with biting the breasts of his female victims.

- - - - - - - - - - - - - - - - - - - - - - - - - - - - - - - - - - - - - - - - - -

**As a result, Boden became known as "The Vampire Rapist" and was the first killer and rapist to be convicted in North America by the use of forensic orthodontic evidence.**

Wayne Clifford Boden (raised in Dundas, Ontario, Canada) sought his first female victims amongst the S & M community of Montreal, combining his love for sadistic sex with an intense attraction to female breasts. Unsatisfied with merely nipping his victims's breasts with his teeth, Boden ripped and tore them to draw blood and soon developed a taste for the blood he sucked from his victims's mutilated breasts. He murdered four women, all of whom he was familiar with – three in Montreal, and one 2,500 miles away, in Calgary.

Boden's first victim was Shirley Audette from Montreal. She was strangled, her breasts bitten and torn savagely, but with no sign of a struggle; her clothing was intact and her blouse buttons had been carefully unfastened. Shirley's boyfriend told detectives that Shirley had wanted to try "rough sex". Boden, it was established, lived in the same apartment block as Shirley and they frequented the same nightclubs.

A month later, Marielle Archambault became Boden's second victim. Again, Marielle enjoyed the same social scene as Boden whom she knew as "Bill". Marielle had been raped and strangled, her breasts bitten and bruised, her tights and bra ripped off.

Two months after killing Marielle, Boden struck again. Jean Way had known Boden for over a year before he murdered her. Boden left Jean's strangled, raped body naked on her bed – her breasts unharmed. Jean had tried desperately to fight him off, tearing at him with her nails. During the frenzied assault, Jean's boyfriend banged on the door causing Boden to flee the scene before he could bite and suck her breasts.

More than a year passed before Boden committed his fourth and final attack in Calgary. Elizabeth Anne Porteous was, like Boden, a native of Dundas, Ontario and they knew each other from home. Elizabeth was strangled and raped, her breasts and neck mauled by savage bites and her apartment wrecked as she fought for her life. Crucial clues had been left though – bite marks on her body and a single broken cufflink.

On the night Elizabeth was killed, witnesses saw her travelling in a blue Mercedes driven by a "flashy" man. The police spotted the car parked near the murder scene, and arrested the driver. It was Boden.

Boden's fate was sealed by his bite marks. An orthodontist compared the marks on Elizabeth's breasts and neck with Boden's teeth and a match was confirmed. This orthodontic evidence convicted him of the murder of Elizabeth Anne Porteous and the three Montreal victims. He was tried and convicted of all four murders in Montreal and sentenced to three life terms in 1972. He was imprisoned at the Kingston Penitentiary, Ontario, but died of skin cancer in Kingston General Hospital in March 2006.

*LEFT: Forensic odontology became an important weapon in law enforcement following the successful conviction of Wayne Boden*

# Jerry Brudos

Jerry Brudos was the youngest of four sons born to a mother desperate for a girl. Consequently, she would dress her young son in girl's clothing.

- - - - - - - - - - - - - - - - - - - - - - - - - - - - - - - - - - - - - - - - - - -

**Brudos's mother abused, belittled and treated her youngest son with disdain. It might come as little surprise to learn that, by the age of five years, Brudos had developed a fetish for women's shoes. He found and played with his first pair of high-heeled shoes in a local scrapyard.**

As Brudos (born in Webster, South Dakota, in 1939) developed, so did his fetish – he tried to steal the shoes belonging to his primary school teacher – but it also expanded to include women's underwear. As a child, he stole lacy underwear from his female neighbours but, as a teenager, Brudos fixated increasingly on women and what they wore, becoming a stalker. Any woman he took a particular interest in would be knocked over and strangled unconscious; Brudos would then flee the scene with her shoes and he spent a great deal of time trying to explain his activities to psychotherapists.

At 17, his larcenist lingerie and footwear fetish took a disturbing turn. He abducted a young woman at knifepoint and beat her severely. He stripped her naked and photographed her. He was later arrested and incarcerated in a psychiatric ward where he was evaluated and found to be suffering from schizophrenia. His developing sexual revenge fantasies were assessed and found to be focused on his hatred of his mother – and women in general – and yet Brudos married a young girl. He required his new bride to do the housework wearing nothing but a pair of high-heeled shoes. As his naked wife cleaned and vacuumed their house, Brudos took pornographic photographs.

Suffering "blackouts" and migraine headaches, Brudos discovered that nocturnal expeditions to steal women's shoes and underwear relieved his symptoms. He stored his "trophies" in his garage and, if his wife wished to enter the garage, she had to seek his permission via an intercom he had set up for the purpose.

Brudos's fixation on women became murderous and he eventually beat and strangled four women to death. Each murder was celebrated by donning a pair of high-heeled shoes and masturbating.

Witnesses had reported observing a big man dressed as a woman in the vicinity of the crime scenes, which led police officers to Brudos who confessed to the murders. His garage was searched and found to contain gory "trophies" of his kills; police found a pair of amputated breasts that he used as paper weights. Having murdered an encyclopedia saleswoman who visited his house, he had stored her body in his garage and used it to model his collection of women's underwear. He also amputated her left foot, which he used to model high-heeled shoes.

Brudos received a life sentence for his brutal crimes but, as a prisoner, he was allowed to keep catalogues of women's shoes – which he considered his pornography – in his cell.

In March 2006, Jerry Brudos died in prison from liver cancer.

*ABOVE: Women's high-heeled shoes became an obsession with Jerry Brudos and transformed him into a serial killer*

# John Norman Collins

John Norman Collins's early life was uneventful and normal. He dated girls regularly, was well liked within his community, and people described him as the archetypal polite young man.

- - - - - - - - - - - - - - - - - - - - - - - - - - - - - - - - - - - - - - - - - -

**Collins was an honours student, and excelled at American Football and baseball and – as a sportsman – was popular with Co-Ed girls. Although his girlfriends described him as respectful and nice, they also reported that he appeared strangely angry most of the time and could be sexually aggressive.**

John Collins was born in Windsor, Ontario, Canada, on 17th June 1947. When he arrived to study at Eastern Michigan University the "Co-Ed Murders" began to materialise. Between 1967 and 1969, the Ann Arbor community in Michigan was terrorised as young female students were stalked, raped, mutilated and murdered by a rapacious serial killer who acquired the nickname, the "Co-Ed Killer".

The first victim was a student at Eastern Michigan University, Mary Fleszar, whose rotting corpse was discovered on an abandoned farm. She had suffered multiple stab wounds, and her hands and feet had been amputated and taken away. Two days later, after the body had been removed from the crime scene, a young man arrived at the local mortuary requesting permission to photograph the body but his request was refused by angry staff. Unfortunately, the members of mortuary staff who had encountered the young man were unable to provide a clear description of him.

The murders continued unabated. Young women were stabbed, shot, strangled and beaten. The killings caused a public outcry, and the police appeared powerless to stop the predatory killer so a psychic was drafted in to assist the investigation but provided no help at all.

Good police work and evidence provided by witnesses began to place Collins at the crime scenes. However, when questioned, Collins provided plausible explanations that were, at first, believed by detectives. The breakthrough they needed came with the brutal killing of Karen Sue Beineman, who had been strangled and beaten to death. The manager of a wig shop, who had been serving Karen Sue shortly before her abduction and murder, was asked by the victim to look at a young man sitting on a motorcycle. Karen Sue had accepted a lift from the man but, not feeling entirely comfortable with her decision, had taken the precaution of informing the older woman. The man was subsequently identified as Collins.

Detectives began to build an evidential and forensic case against Collins. They discovered that he was considered "oversexed", had gained a reputation for sexual harassment and violence against women and was known to be obsessed with bodily mutilation and gore. Collins's arrest, trial and conviction was finally brought about by

the investigative actions of the killer's own uncle, David Leik. The Michigan State Trooper brought his suspicions about his nephew to the attention of the law enforcement authorities and Collins was eventually arrested.

On 19th August 1970, John Norman Collins went to trial. He was convicted and sentenced to life imprisonment with no possibility of parole. Collins continues to serve out his sentence in the Marquette Branch Prison, in Marquette, Michigan.

*ABOVE: John Norman Collins arrives at the Washtenaw County Courthouse*

*OPPOSITE: Police inspect the spot along a rural road where the body of one of Collins's victims was found by a motorist*

# Richard Speck

Richard Speck had a troubled upbringing and was systematically, physically and verbally abused by his alcoholic stepfather. He did poorly in school and dropped out when he was 16 years old.

- - - - - - - - - - - - - - - - - - - - - - - - - - - - - - - - - - - - - - - - - - - - - - - - - -

**He started drinking and was in and out of prison for burglary, forgery and assault, once attacking a woman with a carving knife. Having trouble holding down a job in Texas, he eventually moved to Chicago where his sister lived. Though his sister tried to help him find work, drunken fights with employers left Speck jobless and in need of cash.**

On the evening of 13th July 1966, Richard Speck broke into a nurse's dormitory at 2319 East 100th Street in Chicago, Illinois. While Speck only wanted to burgle the house, high on drugs and alcohol, he ended up holding nine student nurses hostage then systematically murdering them one by one.

Gloria Davy, Patricia Matusek, Nina Jo Schmale, Pamela Wilkening, Suzanne Farris, Mary Ann Jordan, Merlita Gargullo, Valentina Pasion and Cora Amurao lived together in the town house on 2319 East 100th Street. Five of them were home when Speck broke in. He threatened them with a knife and ordered them to hand over their money. A drunken Gloria Davy returned home from a date and stumbled onto the scene. When she screamed, Speck began tying up all the women with torn bed sheets and the violence only escalated. Ann Jordan and Suzanne Farris came in later to see Speck standing over Pamela Wilkening. They ran through the house but Speck caught them, strangled them and stabbed them and then one by one, he murdered the remaining women. Gloria, who fell unconscious, was raped then murdered. Only Cora Amurao, who managed to hide under the bed, survived. She stayed there until 6.00 am the following morning, then ran to the window and screamed that all her friends were dead.

When the police first arrived, they could not believe what they saw. There were bloody hand-prints on the doors and the blood was so thick on the carpet that the officer's shoes sank into it. Several officers had to go outside to vomit. Based on the description provided by Amurao, police were able to identify Speck as the murderer and began a citywide manhunt, splashing his face across every newspaper.

Speck, after fleeing the house, had gone home, cleaned up and went out drinking. His binge lasted four days, during which time he severed an artery on a broken wine bottle and attempted suicide. His drinking buddy recognised Speck from the newspapers and anonymously called the police, although no police car was sent to collect him. An ailing Speck was eventually taken to Cook County Hospital, but not identified as the murderer until a nurse noticed his distinctive tattoo. He was found guilty on eight counts of murder, although countless more attacks and murders have also been attributed to Speck, and sentenced to the death penalty. This was later commuted to life in prison and he died of a heart attack in 1991. His family refused to claim the body.

*LEFT: Richard Speck arrives at the courthouse for trial*

*OPPOSITE: The bloody crime scene of one of the infamous Chicago Nurse murders*

# Edmund Kemper

Edmund Kemper was a genius with an IQ of 145, but he was deeply troubled and earned himself the nickname "Big Ed the Co-Ed Butcher".

----------------------------------------

**As a child, Kemper was known to torture animals and acted out bizarre sexual rituals with his sister's dolls by cutting off their heads while demonstrating a growing fascination for dark "gas chamber" fantasy.**

Edmund Kemper (born in Burbank, California, in 1948) loathed his mother – a violent, mentally ill alcoholic who called him "hulk" and "weirdo" – who forced him to sleep in a locked basement because she firmly believed Kemper was capable of raping his younger sister.

In 1963, Kemper was sent to live with his paternal grandparents on their ranch in California. Here he called his grandfather "senile", and condemned his grandmother for emasculating the males living under her roof. After an argument with his grandmother, he seized a gun and calmly blew her brains out. When his grandfather returned from the shops, Kemper shot him dead in the driveway. He told police officers he had "... just wanted to see what it felt like to kill Grandma".

Aged just 15, Kemper was committed to a secure psychiatric hospital for five years. He grew to be 6ft 9in tall and weighed 22 stone and, upon release, against medical advice having been diagnosed as a paranoid schizophrenic, he was placed in his mother's care.

Kemper's mother got a job at Santa Cruz University and gave him a campus pass, which was ultimately to have terrible consequences. After violent arguments with his mother, he would go out looking for girls with whom to take out his pent up rage and sexual frustration. In nine months, he murdered six female students. Charming and pleasant, he offered them lifts then drove them to isolated places and stabbed, strangled or smothered them. He took the bodies back to his apartment, where he stripped them and took pornographic photographs. He then decapitated them, raped their headless bodies and performed oral sex with their severed heads. He cut open their stomachs and copulated with the open wounds. He slowly dissected their corpses, savouring the eroticism, having sex with various body parts, then disposed of them in the wilderness around Santa Cruz. He buried the head of one victim outside his mother's bedroom window and later said: "She always wanted people to look up to her."

Inevitably, Kemper finally turned on his mother. He battered her to death with a claw hammer before raping her corpse, cutting off her head and performing oral sex with it. Her severed head was then used as a dartboard. He cut out her tongue and vocal cords, feeding them into the garbage disposal unit, but it spat the tissue back into the sink. He said: "That seemed appropriate, as much as she'd bitched and screamed and yelled at me over so many years." He then phoned her best friend, met up with her and beat her to death with a brick before having frenzied sex with her body.

When tried in 1973, Kemper pleaded "not guilty" on grounds of insanity, but was found guilty on eight counts of murder. Kemper requested death by torture, but received eight life sentences. He remains incarcerated in the California Medical Facility in Vacaville.

*LEFT: Edmund Kemper, towering above police officers, is escorted into court in April 1973*

# Manuel Delgado Villegas

Manuel Delgado Villegas's mother died during a traumatic childbirth, which resulted in Delgado and his older sister being raised by their grandmother in Catalonia.

- - - - - - - - - - - - - - - - - - - - - - - - - - - - - - - - - - - - - - - - -

**When he turned 18, Delgado joined the Spanish Legion where he learned hand-to-hand combat techniques. The "golpe mortal" (deathly blow) later became one of his methods for killing.**

Following his departure from the army, Manuel Delgado Villegas (born on 25th January 1943) lived a nomadic lifestyle, wandering along the Mediterranean coastline where he was arrested several times for minor crimes including theft. His first confirmed murder occurred in 1964 when he attacked a man who was sleeping on a bench in Garraf near Barcelona. After bludgeoning him on the head with a rock, he went on to steal the victim's wallet and watch.

Delgado's victims were men and women whom he aimed to rob or rape. Whether they were young, old, heterosexual or homosexual was irrelevant to him and many of his victims suffered their deaths as a result of Delgado's rage. A passing comment or insult may have been all it took for him to launch an attack; none of the murders, it was later discovered, were premeditated. His method of killing involved the victims being strangled, suffocated or beaten to death and two of Delgado's victims showed evidence of necrophilia.

His second victim was a French student who was staying in a holiday resort in Can Planas. Delgado suffocated her with a pillow, stabbed her in the back with a stiletto and then proceeded to rape her once she was dead.

Delgado's killing spree continued until 1971, claiming the lives of at least six further people.

The authorities were unaware that the same person was perpetrating the murders as they occurred across various locations throughout Spain. Delgado was finally caught when Antonia Rodriguez Relinque, a 38-year-old woman, went missing. Local residents confirmed that Delgado had been seen in her company on several occasions and he was subsequently questioned over her disappearance. Her body was discovered in a secluded spot and Delgado admitted to murdering her by strangling her with her leggings. He also confessed that he had returned to have sex with her corpse for three consecutive nights claiming that: "...dead or alive, she was still his girlfriend".

Once detained by police, Delgado was forthcoming in providing them with details of all the murders he had committed. He claimed to have killed 48 people throughout France, Spain and Italy. However, there was no trial or proper conviction as he was placed in a mental institution after being diagnosed with a severe mental disorder. Delgado died in hospital on 2nd February 1998.

*ABOVE: Delgado learned his deadly trade during his time with the Spanish Legion*

# Jack the Stripper

Between 1964 and 1965 a series of murders known as the "nude murders" took place in the Hammersmith area of London.

**The perpetrator was never captured but became known as "Jack the Stripper" because of the manner in which he left his victims to be discovered. His nickname derived from the similarities to the Jack the Ripper murders in the Victorian era due to all the victims being known prostitutes.**

There are six confirmed victims of the Stripper case, although it is believed that two further murders may also be linked. His modus operandi resulted in the victim being raped or sexually assaulted, then strangled and stripped naked with the exception of either one or both stockings.

The first victim, Hannah Tailford, was found dead near Hammersmith Bridge. There was evidence of strangulation and her semen-stained underwear had to be removed from her throat. With several teeth missing, this suggested that the Stripper had rammed the underwear into the victim's mouth with violent force.

The Stripper struck again claiming the life of Irene Lockwood in April and, within three weeks, moved on to his third victim, a 22-year-old woman named Helen Barthelemy. It was at this crime scene that police investigators were able to uncover their first piece of crucial evidence; paint flecks used in automotive factories was found upon the corpse, suggesting that the killer was an employee of a motor manufacturer at a nearby business and two further bodies were discovered with the paint flecks on them.

The paint was traced to an electrical transformer behind a trading estate only metres away from where the body of Bridget O'Hara, the Strippers sixth victim, was discovered in an outdoor storage shed. Her body showed signs of having been stored in a warm environment and the transformer was the likely source.

Scotland Yard detectives interviewed nearly 7,000 suspects in relation to the nude murders but to no avail. In an attempt to lure out the killer and obtain any witness testimonials, the police held a public news conference announcing that their search had been narrowed down to a possible 10 suspects. There were no further murders following the news conference leading to much speculation surrounding the sudden cessation in the killer's activities. Various theories suggested the murderer's possible suicide or that he fled the London area altogether.

*BELOW: A map showing the close proximity to the River Thames in London where at least six young women had been found murdered*

*OPPOSITE: Police officers at the murder scene where Hannah Tailford's body was found*

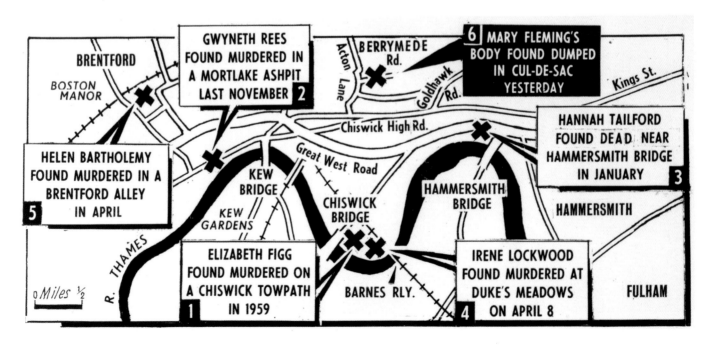

# Boston Strangler

A series of violent murders in early 1960s Boston, Massachusetts, left young women terrified for their lives, some going so far as to move from the area to avoid a potentially gruesome death.

From 1962 to 1964, 13 women ranging in age from 19 to 85 were sexually assaulted and strangled to death with nylon stockings. There was no sign of forced entry into their homes, indicating that the women felt they could trust the murderer. First dubbed the "Mad Strangler of Boston", the killer became known more simply as the "Boston Strangler", but his identity remains unclear to this day.

ABOVE: An aerial view of the exhumation of Albert
DeSalvo's remains in July 2013

OPPOSITE: Albert DeSalvo is captured in February 1967

In October 1964, a woman who had been sexually assaulted by a man posing as a detective identified 33-year-old Albert DeSalvo as her attacker. After DeSalvo was arrested and charged with the rape, he confessed to a fellow inmate that he was the Boston Strangler. Despite inconsistencies in his later confession to police, and a lack of physical evidence, DeSalvo was able to give details of the murders which had not been made public.

There is evidence both for and against DeSalvo. Details of DeSalvo's confession could be corroborated by the police – he could draw floor plans of every victim's apartment; he knew there was a notebook under a victim's bed; he could describe the brand of cigarettes smoked by another. In addition, there was never another confirmed Boston Strangler murder after DeSalvo's arrest.

However, DeSalvo's family and friends, as well as some police officers, could not believe the small time crook could be capable of such vicious attacks. Witnesses who had seen the Strangler enter the victims's apartments could not identify DeSalvo as the man they saw. Cigarettes found in victims's apartments were not the brand they smoked, and DeSalvo himself was a non-smoker. Most importantly, there was no physical evidence to link DeSalvo to the crime scenes. A psychiatrist reported that DeSalvo wanted to be the Boston Strangler in order to gain attention and as a means to raise money for his family. Another

professional confirmed that DeSalvo had an exceptional memory that allowed him to remember the details he gave in his confession based on what he read in newspapers and his own research of the victims's apartments during his time as a burglar.

DeSalvo was never charged with any of the Boston Strangler murders but given a life sentence for a series of rapes. He was stabbed to death in prison in November 1973, but questions still circulate as to who the Boston Strangler really was. DNA evidence examined in 2001 seemed to suggest that DeSalvo was not the man who sexually assaulted the final victim, Mary Sullivan, but this was dis-proven with the exhumation of DeSalvo's remains in 2013.

There are several theories that the Boston Strangler murders were committed by multiple assailants, possibly as many as six. The modus operandi were different in many of the cases and the murder of Patricia Bissette, victim eight, was much gentler – the killer tucking her into bed – than others like Mary Sullivan, who was sodomised with a broom handle. No one has ever been charged with the Boston Strangler murders.

# Graham Young

From a young age, Graham Young was fascinated with chemistry and poisons. After passing the 11 plus, Young's father bought him a chemistry set, thereby fuelling his strange obsession and creating the "St Albans Poisoner".

**In 1961, aged 14, Young started lacing his family's food with various poisons. He would even forget which foods he had poisoned and fall ill himself. After his stepmother died in 1962, the family grew suspicious of Young's unusual behaviour and sent him to a psychiatrist who then recommended they contact the police.**

After being arrested for the attempted murder of his family, Young was sent to Broadmoor Hospital, where he was diagnosed with a personality disorder and schizophrenia.

At just 14 years old, he was Broadmoor's youngest patient since 1885, yet his passion for poison never waned. A few weeks after he

*ABOVE: Graham Young*

was admitted, a fellow inmate died of cyanide poisoning. Although no cyanide could be found, Young explained to the staff how cyanide could be extracted from the laurel bushes surrounding the hospital's property, but it was never proved if the young inmate was responsible. On another occasion, the staff's coffee was spiked with bleach and Young, again, was suspected and for his part seemed determined to poison whenever he was given the slightest opportunity. However, he was released in February 1971 after a psychiatrist decided he had been cured of his obsession.

Young took immediate advantage. He found a job as a storeroom assistant at John Hadland Laboratories where his colleagues were unaware of his penchant for poisons. All Broadmoor had told his employer was that Young had recovered from a psychological illness, even though this was a firm that routinely worked with thallium. Young never stole poison from work though, because he secured plenty of supplies in London by using a fake ID.

After Young volunteered to make tea for his workmates, his colleagues began falling ill. Storeroom manager Bob Egle, along with several other employees, began suffering from diarrhoea, fevers and burning sensations in the throat. Their symptoms would disappear after taking time off, only to return once they returned to work. In July, Egle suffered from severe numbness and paralysis before dying. After his death, employees continued to suffer. Vomiting, intense pain and hair loss were all common complaints. Local doctors were stumped. A stomach virus had swept through the area a few months prior, and many believed it was this "Bovingdon bug" that was to blame. However, after a second employee died, an official investigation began.

When Young bragged to a colleague about his knowledge of chemicals and toxins, the police were informed and Young's true past was revealed. The police arrested him in November 1971. Young had thallium in his pockets and more poison was found at his flat, along with a diary that documented every poisoning he had done along with the doses, their effects, who he wanted to kill and who he wanted to live.

Young was found to have poisoned over 70 people and was sentenced to life in prison. He died in Parkhurst Prison in 1990 of natural causes.

# Eric Edgar Cooke

Eric Edgar Cooke, "The Night Caller", was one of Australia's most notorious serial killers.

- - - - - - - - - - - - - - - - - - - - - - - - - - - - - - - - - - - - - - - - - - -

**He was born on 25th February 1931, in Perth, Western Australia, the eldest of three children, with a cleft palate and a hare lip. With his facial deformity and mumbling speech, he had the types of disabilities that made him a direct target for bullies.**

Cooke's father was a violent alcoholic and a wife beater. Cooke was beaten brutally by his father while trying to protect his mother, suffering lasting brain damage and headaches that plagued him all his life. He left school at 14 to support his family and was quickly drawn in to petty crime. His criminal offences escalated and, at 18 years old, he was sent to prison for three years.

Full of anger at his perceived mistreatment by the world around him, Cooke went on a murderous rampage on 27th January 1963 – Australia Day – armed with a stolen rifle, where he terrorised the streets of Perth.

Cooke's first victims were a middle-aged couple sitting in a car. The bullet passed through the woman's hand, and through the man's neck. Next, Cooke shot a man in the head, leaving him permanently disabled. A retired grocer, George Walmsley, was next. He was shot dead when he opened his door to the gunman. The final casualty was John Sturkey, a 19-year-old student and Queen's Scout. Sturkey was shot as he slept on the veranda of a boarding house.

After this night of fear and bloody mayhem, the residents of Perth broke the habit of a lifetime; they started locking their doors and cars at night.

But, Cooke wasn't finished with them yet. There then followed a series of random shootings, stranglings, stabbings and fatal hit-and-runs using stolen cars. He strangled a woman to death with the flex of a bedside lamp, then he raped her corpse, dragged her body onto a neighbour's lawn and penetrated her sexually with an empty whiskey bottle.

During the hunt for "The Night Caller", 30,000 males over the age of 12 were fingerprinted, and 60,000 rifles were located and test-fired. The breakthrough came following the fatal shooting of babysitter Shirley McLeod in August 1963. A rifle was observed hidden in a bush, and police replaced it with a similar weapon, which they tied to the bush with fishing line. They captured Cooke 17 days later when he returned to collect it and ballistic testing confirmed that this was the weapon used to kill Shirley McLeod.

Cooke confessed to eight murders, 14 attempted murders and more than 250 burglaries. These included two murders for which innocent men had been wrongly convicted and imprisoned. At his trial, Cooke pleaded "not guilty" on the grounds of insanity. However, the director of the state mental health services testified that Cooke was sane, but had a "chronic long-standing resentment against society".

He was convicted of wilful murder, and sentenced to be executed by hanging. Cooke was the last man to face the gallows in Western Australia, on 26th October 1964.

*ABOVE: Eric Edgar Cooke's grave in plot 409, Fremantle Cemetery*

# Peter Manuel

From 1956 to 1958, horrific murders across Scotland were attributed to the unidentified "Beast of Birkenshaw".

-------------------------------------------------------------------------------------------

**Seventeen-year-old Anne Kneilands was the first, murdered in January 1956. She had been waiting for her date, but he failed to show up. Instead, she was stalked across a golf course, raped and then beaten to death with a piece of iron. The suspect was Peter Manuel, a known sex offender, who had been working in the area for a utilities company. However, after Manuel's father provided a false alibi, there wasn't enough evidence to convict, leaving him free to kill again.**

Manuel, born to Scottish parents in New York, returned with his family to Scotland when he was five years old. He was often bullied and, by the age of 10, was already known to the police as a petty thief. His crimes escalated as he got older, and he committed several sexual attacks and rapes before graduating to murder with Anne's death in 1956. There would be little commonality between the victims or how the murders were executed. Sometimes it was following rape, sometimes after a burglary. Nine months after killing Anne, Manuel broke into the home of Marion and William Watt in the middle of the night, shooting and killing Marion, the couple's daughter and Marion's sister. William, who was not home at the time, was arrested and, although released due to lack of evidence, remained the prime suspect until Manuel confessed to the murders in 1958.

Soon after the Watt murders, Manuel was incarcerated for burglary. Upon his release in 1957, Manuel wasted no time in killing again. This time it was 36-year-old taxi driver Sydney Dunn whom he encountered while looking for work in Newcastle upon Tyne. He shot Dunn at close range then slit his throat. Three weeks later, he killed another girl in a fashion similar to Anne Kneilands. As 17-year-old Isabelle Cooke left her home for a grammar school dance, Manuel stalked her, raped her and strangled her before burying her body in a field. By now, Manuel's killing spree was coming to an end, but not before he would murder another family. On 1st January 1958, Manuel broke into the home of Peter and Doris Smart. Like the Watt's, Manuel shot both Peter and Doris and their 10-year-old son, Michael. This time, Manuel stayed at their house for a week, eating their food, driving their car and even feeding the family cat.

Although the police suspected Manuel of many of the murders, it was not until he was caught using banknotes stolen from the Smart family that there was enough evidence to arrest him. Manuel denied everything until his mother came to the police station, imploring him to confess. He did, not only to the Smarts's but a dozen other murders as well. He was convicted of killing nine people, though it's suspected he may have killed as many as 18. He was hanged at Barlinnie Prison in July 1958.

*RIGHT: Peter Manuel*

*OPPOSITE: Police search the river at Uddingston following the murder of the Smart family*

# Joachim Kroll

Born in 1933, Joachim Kroll grew up in Germany during the Second World War (1939–1945). One of many children, he possessed an IQ of just 76 and suffered from prolific bed-wetting.

**He would grow up to become "Uncle Joachim", an unusual but child-loving man, trusted by the parents of the neighbourhood. What those parents didn't know was that Uncle Joachim was also the notorious Ruhr Cannibal, a man who strangled, raped and ate those same trusting children.**

Whatever restraints had been holding back Kroll's murderous tendencies vanished after his mother's death in 1955. Three weeks later, he lured 19-year-old runaway Irmgard Strehl into a barn, stabbed her in the neck then raped her. Afterwards, he strangled and disembowelled her. Irmgard would become one of his oldest victims. The majority would be much younger, including his next, 12-year-old Erika Schuletter, whom he strangled and raped a year later.

After settling in Duisburg in 1957, Kroll started making trips to nearby towns to hunt down his victims. He found favourite places to perform his murders and often would only kill if he could do so in that same place. As a result, there were several years between his murders but his methods were varied. Most often he would strangle his victims then, after they were dead, rape their corpses. He even kept rubber sex dolls that he would use at home after each murder.

It was with his fourth victim, 16-year-old Manuela Knodt, that he became a cannibal, slicing flesh from her buttocks and thighs.

He would later say that he chose to do this because he enjoyed the taste and because meat was so expensive and scarce.

Kroll continued to kill in the 1960s and 1970s, earning himself the nicknames the "Ruhr Cannibal", "Ruhr Hunter" and "Duisburg Man-Eater". Because there were many other killers operating in the area at the time, and because he killed so sparingly, Kroll evaded capture for decades. Innocent men were even convicted for some of Kroll's murders and eventually committed suicide despite their innocence. It would be the murder of his youngest victim, four-year-old Marion Ketter, that finally saw Kroll's downfall.

Marion disappeared from a neighbourhood playground in July 1976. Shortly after, Kroll told a neighbour that the communal toilet was blocked with "guts". When the man discovered blood in the toilet, he ran out into the street and found police officers who were searching for the small child. When the police investigated the toilet's contents, they discovered it contained the internal organs of a human child. The police confronted Kroll. He lied at first and said it was the remains of a rabbit but later admitted he had been preparing human meat. They searched his flat and made a gruesome discovery – a child's hand cooking in a pot of stew. More human flesh was found in the refrigerator and freezer.

A remorseless Kroll was immediately arrested and eventually sentenced to life in prison for eight murders, though his true total is cited as 15 or more. He died in prison of a heart attack in 1991.

*LEFT: The prison at Rheinbach, where Joachim Kroll lived the last years of his life*

# Ed Gein

Edward (Ed) Theodore Gein, born in 1906, was strongly influenced by his Lutheran mother, Augusta, who read to him from the Bible each afternoon from the Old Testament about murder, death and divine retribution.

- - - - - - - - - - - - - - - - - - - - - - - - - - - - - - - - - - - - - - - - - - - - -

**Apart from going to school, the remainder of Gein's time was spent doing chores on the family farm. He was discouraged from making friends – even punished for it – and had little chance to progress any social skills.**

Gein's older brother Henry was particularly worried about their mother's influence over Ed and often said so, which greatly upset his younger brother. In May 1944, Henry Gein was found dead on the family farm, but foul play was not suspected (although it came to light in later years).

Gein's mother suffered two strokes the following year and died, leaving him alone on the farm and utterly devastated. He boarded up most of the house and began living in one room next to the kitchen where he developed an intense interest in Nazi atrocities as well as cults and cannibalism.

When the owner of the local hardware shop Bernice Worden went missing in Plainfield, Wisconsin, in 1957, Gein found himself under suspicion because the last receipt she'd written had been for some anti-freeze that he was known to have purchased. The victim was found on Gein's farm in a shed. She had been shot and hung upside down. Once dead, her body had been badly mutilated and decapitated. While shocked to find the victim, police were to find other body parts, which would prove equally as disturbing. As an investigation got underway, skulls were found on Gein's bedstead, as well as skulls that had been made into bowls. In addition, a belt made from women's nipples, a lampshade made from human skin, the head of another victim, Mary Hogan, female genitalia and 10 female heads with the top of the skull sawn off, were found around the farm. It was a shocking find. It transpired that between 1947 and 1952, Gein had made up to 40 visits to three graveyards where he had exhumed the bodies of women he described as resembling his mother. After her death, he had decided that he wished to have a sex change and had been in the process of making a woman's bodysuit for himself from human skin. During questioning, Gein admitted to robbing nine graves and shooting local tavern owner Mary Hogan, who had been missing for three years.

Gein's case came to court in November 1957, but he was declared unfit for trial by reason of insanity and was incarcerated at the Central State Hospital for the Criminally Insane. He died of a cancer-related illness in 1984. The book and film "Psycho", as well as "Silence of the Lambs" and other creations, are said to have been inspired by Gein's horrific crimes.

*LEFT: Ed Gein leads police around the crime scene*

# John Straffen

John Straffen was one of the most notorious child murderers in British history. Born in Hampshire in 1930, mental illness ran in his family.

**Straffen, aged nine, had no comprehension of the difference between "right" and "wrong". He was certified a mental defective with a mental age of six, and sent to a residential school where he became a loner, with a tendency to resist authority and a love of strangling animals.**

At the age of 16, Straffen was evaluated with a mental age of nine and was reported to the police for assaulting a 13-year-old girl. He had put his hand over her mouth and said: "What would you do if I killed you? I have done it before." Six weeks after the assault, Straffen was found to have strangled five chickens that had belonged to the girl's father. He was arrested for the crime and a string of burglaries to which he had confessed. He was then committed to the Hortham Colony, which rehabilitated mentally ill patients for return to the community. At 21, Straffen found a job in a market garden, was allowed to go on unescorted home visits and, by now, had a mental age of 10.

On his way to the cinema in Bath, he encountered five-year-old Brenda Goddard, who was picking flowers. He befriended her, telling her he knew where there were some much better flowers. Straffen led her into a wood, strangled her, smashed her head against a stone to make sure she was dead, and then went on to the cinema. Police questioned Straffen, alongside other men, about the murder but, not being considered violent, he was released. Police officers questioning Straffen's employer about his movements consequently saw him losing his job which deepened his hatred of the police.

On 8th August 1951, he met Cicely Batstone, aged nine, at the cinema. He took her by bus to a meadow called the "Tumps" on the edge of Bath and strangled her to death, but his abduction of Cicely had been witnessed by many people. He was easily identified, and was later arrested at home. He was questioned and confessed to the murders of Cicely and Brenda before being charged with murder and remanded in custody.

He was tried for both murders in 1951, but was found unfit to plead due to insanity and sent to Broadmoor Hospital in Berkshire. On 29th April 1952, Straffen escaped from Broadmoor by jumping over the hospital wall and evading the guards. Within an hour and a half of his escape, he came across five-year-old Linda Bowyer riding her bicycle. He strangled the young child to death before subsequently being recaptured and driven back to Broadmoor. Linda's body was discovered the next day.

Police officers interviewed the killer about the murder of Linda, and he was eventually tried and sentenced to hang, but the death sentence was commuted to life imprisonment. He remained in prison for the next 55 years and died, aged 77, on 19th November 2007 in Frankland Prison in County Durham.

*RIGHT: Brenda Goddard, John Straffen's first victim*

*LEFT: John Straffen being escorted by police officers into Winchester Court House during his murder trial in July 1952*

*LEFT: A police officer guards the crime scene where nine-year-old Cicely Batstone was found murdered*

# John George Haigh

John George Haigh, known as the "Acid Bath Murderer", was convicted of the murders of six people during the 1940s.

-------------------------------------------------------

**He wrongly believed that if there were no bodies, then he could not be convicted of murder and he used sulphuric acid to dispose of the bodies of his victims.**

John George Haigh, born in Stamford, Lincolnshire, in 1909, was brought up by his parents, who were staunch Plymouth Brethren followers, in West Yorkshire. Although it was many years before, like Stephen Griffiths, Haigh attended Queen Elizabeth School in Wakefield. He was an accomplished pianist, although his contact with the "outside" world was limited by his parents, who firmly believed in an austere lifestyle.

Haigh was a petty criminal sacked for stealing from his employer but, in 1934, he married Betty Hamer and was sent to prison for fraud. His wife left him, put their newborn daughter up for adoption and, like the rest of his family, ostracised Haigh from that point on. He moved to London in 1936, but was again jailed for fraud.

Throughout the duration of the Second World War (1939–1945), Haigh was imprisoned a number of times for fraudulent activities. It was while in prison that he dreamt of the perfect murder. At first, he experimented with mice and found that it took just 30 minutes for the small rodent bodies to disappear when placed in acid.

In 1944, Haigh killed his former employer, wealthy William McSwann, before dumping the man's body in a 40-gallon drum. He poured concentrated sulphuric acid over it and left it for two days. When he returned, the body had turned to sludge, which Haigh poured down a manhole.

He murdered McSwann's parents when they became suspicious over their son's disappearance. Haigh sold the family's properties, stole pension cheques and moved into a plush hotel. When gambling debts rendered him short of money, he found another wealthy couple, the Hendersons, and killed them in the same way, disposing of their bodies in acid.

He then lured wealthy widow, Olive Durand-Deacon to his workshop in West Sussex. Mrs Durand-Deacon was a fellow resident of the Onslow Court Hotel. Her friend, Constance Lamb, reported Olive missing and police discovered Haigh's dubious past. At his workshop, they found a dry cleaning receipt for an expensive coat owned by Olive as well as paperwork belonging to the McSwanns and Hendersons.

Haigh was found guilty of the murders and executed by hanging in Wandsworth Prison, London on 10th August 1949.

*LEFT: Police officers sift through the top soil and a pile of burnt rubbish at Crawley, trying to piece together the murder of Mrs Durand-Deacon*

*OPPOSITE: John George Haigh, smiling broadly, is led handcuffed to police into court in March 1949*

# John Christie

John Christie was convicted of murdering his wife in 1953, sentenced to death and hung on 15th July that same year.

- - - - - - - - - - - - - - - - - - - - - - - - - - - - - - - - - - - - - - - - - - -

**He had admitted murder, but pleaded not guilty by reason of insanity before he hid her body under the floorboards of their Notting Hill home in London.**

Christie had fought in the First World War (1914-1918) and had lost the ability to speak for around three years having been exposed to a mustard gas shell explosion. However, Christie's defence lost their argument that the killer was mad because the jury had sat through evidence that eight bodies (all female), including the body of a baby girl, had been found at the Christie's home at 10 Rillington Place. All of Christie's victims had been strangled.

Timothy Evans, a former neighbour of the Christie's, had been executed for the murder of his baby daughter. The charge of murder for his wife was dropped once he was hung in 1950. By the time the bodies of Evan's wife and daughter were found at Rillington Place, and it was established that they had probably fallen foul of Christie, it was far too late for the late bereft husband and father. It is believed that Christie developed a deep hatred for women. He was sexually inadequate and when he married Ethel Waddington, she did little to help the situation. He was known for being violent at work, frequented prostitutes and went to prison several times for theft and violence.

Christie admitted to the death of his first victim, Ruth Fuerst, whom he strangled during sex in August 1943. First, he hid her body under floorboards at Rillington Place, before burying it in the back garden. His second victim, Muriel Eady, inhaled a carbon monoxide substance which Christie administered – having told her it would cure her bronchitis – in October 1948. Once unconscious, the killer raped her before strangling her and burying her in the back garden of his home. Evans accused Christie of the murders of his wife and daughter in late 1949. Christie eventually murdered his own wife in December 1952. Ethel, like the other women and child, was strangled. At the beginning of 1953, he murdered a further three women. He was eventually caught, wandering around close to Putney Bridge in London following the discovery of the bodies at Rillington Place.

*BELOW: John Christie on his way to court in April 1953*

*OPPOSITE: Mrs Hart, the neighbour of serial killer John Christie, points to the spot in the garden of 10 Rillington Place, London, where two of his victims were buried*

# Peter Kürten

The third of 13 children, Peter Kürten's upbringing was so poor and abusive that it was perhaps inevitable that he turned into "The Vampire of Düsseldorf".

**He repeatedly witnessed his sadistic, drunken father sexually abuse his mother and sisters in their shared, one-room apartment. Consequently, Kürten – taking his moral lead from his depraved father – also began to abuse his sisters sexually.**

Peter Kürten was born on 26th May 1883, in the German town of Mülheim am Rhein although the family moved to Düsseldorf in 1894. Having moved to the city, Kürten's criminal offending escalated to include theft and arson. At the age of 12, he started a relationship with another boy and was introduced to the practices of urolagnia and coprophagia (drinking urine and eating faeces). These horrific influences on such a young child would turn Kürten into a cannibal and notorious predator of young children.

ABOVE: A portrait of "The Vampire of Düsseldorf", Peter Kürten

Having come under the poisonous spell of a local dog catcher, Kürten's cruelty to animals developed into a murderous cruelty towards people, and he committed his first known murder in 1913. While burgling a public house he encountered and strangled the landlord's 10-year-old daughter, Christine Kline, to death.

Kürten was conscripted into the German Army in 1914, but the harsh realities caused him to desert. He was captured, and served eight years in prison for desertion. Released in 1921, he met and married a former prostitute but, still enraged at his "unjust" incarceration by the state, commenced his ferocious campaign of sadistic killings – a blood-drenched road that lead to his fatal appointment with the guillotine.

Before his eventual trial, Kürten admitted to 79 offences, and was charged with nine murders and seven attempted murders. Between 1929 and 1930, Kürten undertook a series of especially frenzied attacks on men, women and children. His murder weapons of choice were hammers, scissors and knives. He found murdering people sexually stimulating and, when he stabbed his victims multiple times, he discovered that the erotic thrusting, stabbing action would bring him to sexual climax. The number of stab wounds counted on a victim's corpse reflected the time it took him to achieve orgasm. For his personal sexual gratification, he stabbed a male mechanic 20 times and, having strangled a five-year-old girl, he stabbed her body 36 times with a pair of scissors. The sight of his victims's blood only heightened Kürten's depraved sexual pleasure. On at least one occasion, Kürten is believed to have consumed the blood of a victim, and it was this heinous act that resulted in him being dubbed "The Vampire of Düsseldorf" by the city's appalled press.

Kürten revelled in this mass hysteria and public horror. He contacted a newspaper on 9th November 1929, providing journalists with a map locating the dumped corpse of his latest stab victim – five-year-old Gertrude Albermann. Eventually, aware that the police were closing in, Kürten confessed to his wife that he was "The Vampire of Düsseldorf". He believed that if she turned him in, she would receive a large financial reward. She complied with his wishes, and Kürten surrendered to the police. Having confessed to his multiple crimes, Kürten pleaded guilty at his trial in April 1931. He was convicted and sentenced to death. On 2nd July 1931, Peter Kürten was beheaded on the guillotine in Cologne.

*Opposite: The front page of the 1st December 1929 edition of the French newspaper "Le Petit Journal Illustre" depicts Peter Kürten terrorising the population of Dusseldorf*

# LE PETIT JOURNAL
## ILLUSTRÉ

HEBDOMADAIRE - 40ᵉ Année
61, rue Lafayette, Paris

1ᵉʳ Décembre 1929 - Nᵒ 2032
PRIX : 50 CENTIMES

## LA TERREUR A DUSSELDORF

# Albert Fish

Born in 1870 into a family with a history of mental illness, Hamilton Howard "Albert" Fish, grew up in Washington, D.C.

**He spent much of his early life in an orphanage, due to family circumstances, where he began to enjoy the sadistic treatment meted out. He learned to tolerate pain and saw many young boys committing sexual acts on each other by the time he was nine years old.**

At the age of 20, Fish moved to New York City where he began working as a male prostitute with a penchant for raping young boys, while he spent much of his youth in bathhouses where he could watch boys undressing at his leisure. Despite this, he married in 1898, fathered six children and outwardly gave the impression of a "normal family man".

But, Fish was fascinated by sexual mutilation and continued to molest young boys alongside writing obscene letters to women. He was known to self-harm and suffered hallucinations. However, upon his release from Sing Sing, where he was incarcerated in 1903 for grand larceny, he began mutilating his victims whom he chose from the African-American and disabled communities. Fish believed that these victims would not be missed and he mutilated them with implements

such as a meat cleaver, a handsaw and a butcher's knife.

By 1924, Fish believed that God wanted him to sexually mutilate children. Elsewhere in New York, believing he could make a better life for his family, Edward Budd, 18, advertised for a position in the country in May 1928. It was Fish, pretending to be a farmer who called on the family under the pretext of offering Edward a job. He intended that Edward should be his next victim. However, on returning to the Budd family apartment he met 10-year-old Grace, whom he immediately identified as his victim instead. He convinced the young girl's parents that he was taking his niece to a party that evening and that Grace

*BELOW: More than 50 fingers, legs and other bones were found near this house where Albert Fish murdered Grace Budd*

should go too. The Budd family never saw her again.

Six years later, the family received a letter from Fish describing how he had cut two small boys, aged seven and 11 into little pieces, cooked their flesh and eaten them. The letter then outlined how Fish had killed Grace and cooked and eaten her in the same way. Mrs Budd, who was illiterate, had to listen as the letter was read out to her describing how her daughter had been eaten over the course of nine days. The stationery used to write the letter was eventually traced to Fish's rented room. He was arrested and further cases came to light.

When he died in the electric chair, in January 1936, he was known to have murdered three children and was suspected of the murders of at least six others.

# Henri Désiré Landru

Henri Désiré Landru was sentenced to death in November 1921 following his trial for the murder of 11 victims. He faced the guillotine three months later in Versailles.

**As he stood trial, Landru traced a picture of his kitchen, including the stove where he was accused of burning those he butchered. Many years later, in 1967, a note he had written on the back of the picture was taken to be his confession. It read: "It is not the wall behind which a thing takes place, but indeed the stove in which a thing has been burned".**

Born in 1869, Landru had a relationship with his cousin, with whom he had a child before he married someone else and had four more children. He was sentenced to two years in prison in 1900 after being convicted of fraud, and was in and out of prison seven times over the next 10 years. By 1908, he developed a plan to swindle widows out of their life savings. At the start of World War I in 1914, following separation from his wife, Landru advertised in the lonely hearts columns of Parisian newspapers, claiming to be a widower looking for matrimony. With so many men killed in the Great War, there were many widows willing to answer his "call for love". Working under many aliases, Landru was successful in luring lonely women into his fraudulent scheme, whereby once they had trusted him enough to give him access to all their assets, the horror would begin.

Landru is often cited as being a real-life 20th Century "Bluebeard", based on the mythical story of a man who killed his seven wives, but who suffered a downfall at the hands of a curious, innocent young woman. The Parisian-born killer was a short man, balding with a thick, brown beard, and not typical of the type of man that women were

likely to romance. However, Landru had an irresistibility that many women were drawn to, even though it was hard to define what it was that attracted them. He had a good sense of humour and the ability to seduce, and a large sexual appetite, but he also had a cruel, inhuman side, which would eventually cost 10 women their lives.

It's not known how Landru murdered his victims, but evidence at his Parisian villa suggested that the killings were clean and the women unlikely to have been defiled. However, once dead, Landru dismembered his victims so that he could "burn" the evidence in his humble kitchen stove. The victims were all listed as missing – including the teenage son of one of his victims – which brought the total death toll to 11. It was the use of his aliases that helped him evade the police for so long, but the sister of one of the women he killed decided to try and find her missing sibling. She knew what Landru looked like and where he lived and she persuaded the police to arrest him. Charged with embezzlement, he refused to talk, but eventually police found paperwork relating to all the victims and Landru was charged with murder.

*LEFT: The scene of the murders committed by Henri Desire Landru*

*OPPOSITE: French mass murderer Henri Desire Landru in court, November 1921*

# Karl Denke

Karl Denke, "The Monster of Münsterberg", came from a wealthy farming family and, on the death of his father, used his inheritance to buy a house in town and a butcher's shop.

**On 21ˢᵗ December 1924, a local resident heard cries for help from Denke's house. He found a young man struggling to escape with blood streaming from a deep head wound. Before he collapsed, the victim blurted out that: "'Vatter' Denke" had tried to murder him with an axe.**

Karl Denke (born on 12ᵗʰ August 1870, in Ziebice, Münsterberg, Poland) was arrested and his home and business premises were searched thoroughly by police. They found documents and clothes belonging to 12 different men – tramps, vagrants and vulnerable people released from prisons and hospitals. Officers discovered two large vats of meat, pickling in brine, pots of fat, and a huge heap of bones, waiting to be boiled.

The arrest of the well-loved family butcher known as "Papa Denke", shocked the whole community. The revelation that their kindly, devout church organist was also a serial killer, a cannibal, and a purveyor of human flesh left local people reeling – and his customers sickened.

All the meat recovered from Denke's property was human in origin. The quantity recovered suggested the processed remains of around 40 people. This was confirmed by the discovery of Denke's detailed ledger, in which he systematically recorded the names, butchering dates and body weights of people he had murdered and pickled between 1912 and 1918. It is believed that, during his butchery career, Denke killed and ate at least 42 people.

Denke's shop was found to contain jars of pickled human flesh, equipment for the manufacture of human leather goods and assorted products made from human skin. Denke wasted nothing – he even used the hair from his victims to make shoelaces.

He had found no shortage of buyers for his gruesome merchandise. He hawked his products door-to-door and he carried his meat to the nearby city of Wroclaw, where it was sold in the market. Meat was in short supply, and Denke had many satisfied customers for his pickled "pork" and "fine leather goods".

On the night of his arrest, Denke hanged himself in his cell with his own handkerchief. His suicide denied police investigators and his former neighbours, local residents and shopkeepers an explanation for his actions or motives.

The fact that Denke preyed exclusively upon drifters and vagrants, and not fellow residents of the town has enabled "The Cannibal of Ziebice" to take his place among its local celebrities. In 1999, the Household Equipment Museum in Ziebice organised an exhibition entitled "An ancient iconography of Ziebice". This exhibition included a selection of butchery tools seized from Denke's home and shop in 1924. The exhibits included bloodied knives, axes, leather working tools and a meat grinder.

Aware of the tourism potential of Denke's story, the museum is planning to install a larger Denke exhibit to attract the morbidly curious to Ziebice.

*LEFT: The only known photograph of Karl Denke, taken following his suicide*

# George Joseph Smith

Born in January 1872 in Bethnal Green, London, George Joseph Smith was in trouble with the law from a young age.

---

**Sent to a reformatory at nine years of age, Smith was imprisoned in his twenties for theft and persuading women to steal for him. His penchant for lying, money and women would eventually lead to murder.**

Smith's first, and only legal, marriage occurred in 1898, although he married a second woman, bigamously, just a year later. When his first wife, a maid, was caught stealing from her employers, she implicated Smith in the crimes and they were both incarcerated. After her release, she emigrated to Canada while Smith stole his second wife's savings and simply vanished. Smith continued this pattern, having seven bigamous marriages between 1908 and 1915. In each case, he married under an alias, stole his wife's money, then left. Yet it wasn't until 1915 that he was suspected of murder.

When Alice Burnham Smith, a 25-year-old bride married for less than a month, died in a bathtub in Blackpool in December 1913, it was determined she suffered a "faint" and drowned in her tub. In 1914, when another bride, Margaret Elizabeth Lloyd, was found dead in her tub less than 24 hours after her marriage, the coroner stated that she had suffered some sort of faint and sadly drowned. However, Joseph Crossley, the owner of the boarding house where Alice Smith died noticed the similarities, and sent newspaper clippings with regard to both women's deaths to Detective Inspector Arthur Neil. Neil began an inquiry that would result in Smith's capture and subsequent execution.

Neil discovered that both women had taken out large life insurance policies prior to their deaths – payable to their new husbands. Neil quickly suspected that this was the work of one man and apprehended Smith at his lawyer's office, where his suspicions were quickly affirmed. It was then Neil's job to prove that Smith had murdered his two wives.

Both Alice and Margaret's bodies were exhumed and, while investigating these deaths, a third murder surfaced. Beatrice Mundy, 31, drowned in the bath after a suspected epileptic fit in 1912, five days after she had changed her will, making her husband sole beneficiary. Once Neil confirmed that this husband was indeed Smith, Mundy's body was also exhumed. The results, however, were inconclusive – no sign of violence or poisoning, indication of an instantaneous death and little evidence of drowning.

Baffled by the women's unexplained tests, Neil performed forensic experiments involving each of the deadly bathtubs, using professional women divers to help him determine how, and if, the women could have been forcibly drowned without signs of violence. His experiments proved that it was possible when he nearly killed one of his assistants

ABOVE: George Joseph Smith standing in front of a painted backdrop of the countryside with murder victim Beatrice Mundy, who knew Smith as "Henry Williams"

by pulling her into the tub by her feet, leaving her no time to react. While the evidence was merely circumstantial, it was enough. Smith, whom the media dubbed "The Brides in the Bath Murderer", was convicted of murder and hanged in August 1915.

# H. H. Holmes

Born Herman Webster Mudgett in 1861, Dr Henry Howard Holmes, the name he used as an alias, was one of America's first serial killers, responsible for the deaths of at least 27 people.

- - - - - - - - - - - - - - - - - - - - - - - - - - - - - - - - - - - - - - - - - - - - - - - - - - -

**However, many commentators claim the death toll could be as high as 200 victims. While his father was an abusive alcoholic, it is known that his mother – a devout Methodist – regularly read the Bible to her son. As a young child, after seeing a skeleton, it is believed that Holmes became completely obsessed with death.**

The exact methods of his killings still remain a mystery. He married in 1878 and had a son, two years later, before graduating from medical school at the University of Michigan in 1884. While studying, Holmes stole bodies from the university laboratory and dismembered them. In addition, he collected insurance policies he took out on the deceased, having told the insurance companies that these people had died in accidents.

Under the name of H. H. Holmes, he began a number of dodgy business dealings and married again in 1887 while still married to his first wife. The couple had a daughter, but he married for a third time while still twice married in Colorado in 1894. A woman he then subsequently had an extra-marital relationship with would later become one of his victims.

Prior to this, he bought a drugstore in Chicago in 1885 from an elderly widow and agreed she could remain in the upstairs apartment. She mysteriously disappeared once the loans Holmes had taken out to buy the store could not be repaid. The Englewood neighbourhood in the city was also where Holmes would buy a lot and build his "World Fair" hotel, in time for the World Colombian Exposition of 1893.

The drugstore was relocated to the ground floor of Holmes's "Castle" as the hotel was dubbed, while the upstairs of the building housed his personal office and more than 100 rooms, all without windows, which he purposefully built as a "murder" hotel. Many of the rooms had doors that opened on to brick walls. Others were soundproofed and had gas pipes installed. All Holmes's employees were required to take out insurance policies. While he paid huge premiums for these polices, he was also the named beneficiary.

The hotel contained stairs that led nowhere, a maze of corridors and doors that only opened from the outside. Holmes chose his victims carefully from among his staff, lovers and hotel guests who were lured there from their visits to the Exposition. Some victims were asphyxiated, others were left to suffocate in a huge vault, and virtually all were tortured.

HERMAN WEBSTER MUDGETT *alias* H. H. HOLMES.

*ABOVE: Holmes was convicted of four murders, although he confessed to 27 but there was widespread, and credible, speculation that he could have been responsible for several hundred*

Holmes had a large stretching rack as well as a secret chute, which he used to transport bodies to the hotel's basement. He also had acid pits and two huge furnaces. Some bodies were dissected and their skin removed. With his medical connections, he found selling skeletons and human organs fairly easy but, with the World Fair over and an economic decline engulfing Chicago, Holmes wandered around the United States and Canada for a while before being incarcerated for a swindle in 1894. He then murdered his long-time associate Benjamin Pitezel and three of Pitezel's children. It was these deaths that brought Holmes to justice. He was hanged in Philadelphia County Prison in 1897.

# Thomas Neill Cream

Four years after he was born in Glasgow, Scotland in 1850, Thomas Cream's family emigrated to Quebec in Canada where he proved a promising student.

- - - - - - - - - - - - - - - - - - - - - - - - - - - - - - - - - - - - - - - - - - - - - - - - - -

**However, Cream was forced at gunpoint to marry a young girl, by her family, after it transpired she was pregnant. As the honeymoon ended, Cream travelled to Britain in order to continue his studies in medicine. He did, however, return to Canada long enough to poison his new wife, who died of a "mysterious" illness.**

When Thomas Neill Cream made his way to Edinburgh to further his studies, a woman he had had an affair with was found dead, presumably from poisoning, and he set sail for the United States.

Cream set up a medical practice in Chicago, offering illegal abortions to women working in the city's red light district. A woman died following one of his operations, but he escaped conviction due to a lack of evidence. His dodgy practices continued and, in 1881, he was convicted of the murder of a man named Stott, whose wife had obtained strychnine from Cream. Although she was also accused of murder, the woman who believed her husband had been cheating on her gave evidence against Cream and he was sentenced to life imprisonment. Ten years later, Cream's brother bribed the authorities and he was released and free to travel back to Britain where he moved to Lambeth, in London. He had only been in the capital a matter of days before his next victim died.

Nineteen-year-old prostitute Ellen "Nellie" Donworth was poisoned with strychnine and died on 16th October 1891. Her death was followed by two more and one attempted murder. Cream was undoubtedly a psychopath and misogynist and he chose prostitute Matilda Clover, 27, as his next victim. He attempted to poison another woman in early April 1892, but she was suspicious of the doctor and refused the drinks he tried to tempt her with. Just a few days later, on 11th April 1892, Cream seduced prostitutes Alice Marsh, 21, and Emma Shrivell, 18. The drinks he plied them with left both women dying in agony. By this time, Cream had long gone but he attempted to accuse two respectable doctors of the murders of several women, including Matilda Clover, whose death had originally been recorded as natural causes due to her problems with alcohol.

Police quickly established that the two accused doctors were entirely innocent of the crimes, but realised that they were dealing with a man who had knowledge of murders they hadn't even known had taken place. Calling their unknown perpetrator the "Lambeth Poisoner", police knew they were dealing with a serial killer. Cream met with a New York police official – aware of the case – and showed him around Lambeth and the areas the women had died. The New York official then explained Cream's interest and knowledge of the case to Scotland Yard who immediately put the doctor under surveillance. Cream's earlier conviction was discovered and he was convicted and found guilty of the Lambeth poisonings. He was executed by hanging in November 1892.

*ABOVE: Thomas Neill Cream's last words, rumoured to be "I am Jack", led him to be suspected of the Jack the Ripper murders, despite his having been in jail at the time they were committed*

# Jack the Ripper

The Whitechapel murders were a series of 11 killings that occurred between 3rd April 1888 and 13th February 1891.

- - - - - - - - - - - - - - - - - - - - - - - - - - - - - - - - - - - - - - - - - - - - - - -

**Five of these have been linked to Jack the Ripper and his modus operandi. Jack the Ripper's victims were all female prostitutes who lived and worked in the slums of Victorian London.**

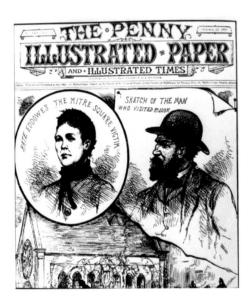

*ABOVE: The press was full of the murder of Kate Eddowes*

George Lusk, the chairman of the Whitechapel Vigilance Committee, received a parcel containing half a human kidney on 16th October that same year. The accompanying note described how the writer had fried and eaten the other half of the organ. The note became known as the "From Hell" letter because of the phrase written in the top right hand corner. There is no evidence that the kidney was in fact the missing organ from Catherine Eddowes.

Mary Jane Kelly fell victim to an atrocious slaughter on 9th November 1888. Unlike the previous women, Kelly was found in a private room, her naked body disembowelled in a vulgar manner. Her neck had a deep cut all the way around to the spine and her face had been disfigured almost beyond recognition with the nose, cheeks, ears and eyebrows being partly removed. Both breasts had been removed with circular incisions, and the kidneys, spleen, intestines, liver and uterus had all been ripped out of her body and placed around it.

All of the victims were seen with an unidentified man just hours before their deaths. The descriptions given often detailed the man to be of dark complexion with a foreign 'shabby-genteel' appearance. Descriptions have also included a man over 40 years old wearing a long dark overcoat. With insufficient evidence, the perpetrator of the Whitechapel murders was never captured and a legend was born.

On 31st August 1888, Mary Ann Nichols was found lying on the ground in front of a gated stable entrance. Nichols's throat had been slashed twice from left to right, which meant that death would have been immediate. The abdominal lacerations included a deep jagged cut and a number of smaller incisions to the right side of her body. The mutilation was done using one instrument, thought to be a knife at least six to eight inches long, which was used by violently slashing downwards into the victim.

On 30th September 1888, The Ripper committed a double murder. Elizabeth Stride was found with a deep wound to her throat but it is thought the Ripper was interrupted by a passer-by as he did not continue with the abdominal butchery seen in his previous victim.

Shortly after, the mutilated body of Catherine "Kate" Eddowes was found. Her throat had been severed from left to right and the intestines ripped out of the abdominal cavity and placed over the left shoulder of the victim. Disfigurement of the face had also taken place with the bridge of her nose, both cheeks and eyelids having been sliced through. Part of one ear and the tip of her nose had been removed completely. Part of the uterus and the left kidney had been extracted and was missing from the murder scene.

*ABOVE: Elizabeth Stride, murdered by Jack the Ripper at Derner Street on 30th September 1888*

*OPPOSITE: Bucks Row (now Durward Street), east London, where the body of Mary Ann Nichols was found lying across the gutter*

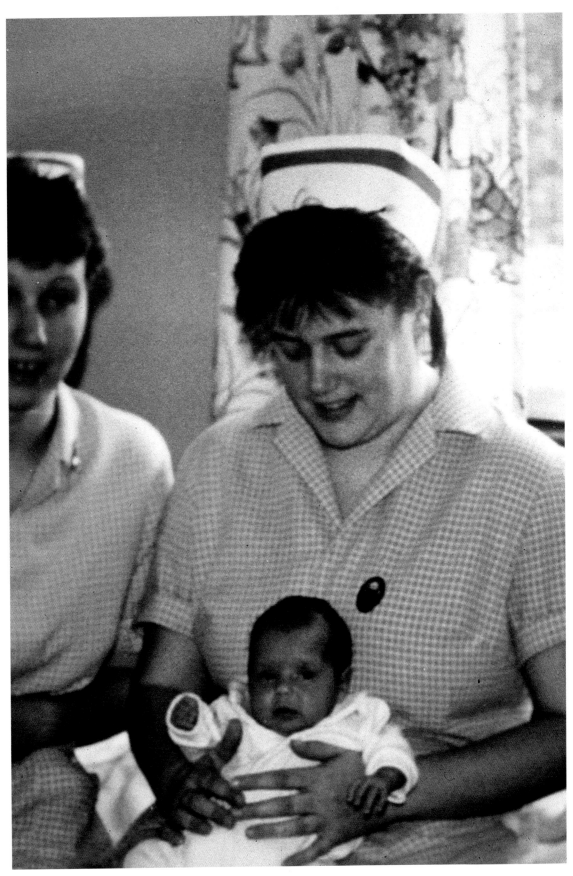

*ABOVE: A picture of innocence, yet nurse Beverley Allitt would
soon become one of Britain's most notorious serial killers*

# Female Killers

# Christine Malèvre

Like Charles Cullen, Christine Malèvre was to become known as the "Angel of Death" for the terminally ill patients she killed with poison while they were in her care.

- - - - - - - - - - - - - - - - - - - - - - - - - - - - - - - - - - - - - - - - - - - - - - - - -

**The former nurse claimed that she killed her victims out of compassion while she worked in Paris, France. Although Malèvre confessed to around 30 murders (some believe there may have been more) in July 1998, she later recanted most of her confessions.**

*ABOVE: Christine Malevre and her lawyer in October 1998*

On 25th July, the same day she was arrested, the nurse tried to kill herself before being taken into custody. She was sentenced to 10 years in prison for six murders in 2003 with a more lenient sentence initially passed due to fact that the patients she helped die, or that she killed, were dying from terminal lung disease. However, her sentence was lengthened to 12 years on appeal in October that year. Malèvre was acquitted of a seventh murder, but banned from the nursing profession for life. She was released in 2007. A report into her criminal activities showed that patients were three times more likely to die while she was on duty, and a further report on her mental state showed that she had a morbid fascination with disease and death.

The debate on euthanasia had been raging in France for some time when the Malèvre case came to trial. Officials had long argued that euthanasia had no place in French society, despite a poll indicating that many French people would not be opposed to it under certain conditions. The debate saw the former nurse described as both a serial killer and a mercy killer.

Christine Malèvre eventually stated that she helped two patients to die at their own request, and that another two deaths were accidents. Family of those murdered by Malèvre claimed that the nurse had never been asked to practise euthanasia on their dying relatives.

# Beverley Allitt

During a 59-day period from February to April 1991, Beverly Allitt became one of Britain's most prolific female serial killers.

- - - - - - - - - - - - - - - - - - - - - - - - - - - - - - - - - - - - - - - - - - - - - - - - - -

**Allitt murdered four children, attempted the murder of three more and caused grievous bodily harm to six others in the children's ward of Grantham and Kesteven Hospital, Lincolnshire. Her victims ranged from seven weeks to 11 years old. At least two victims were injected with high doses of insulin and another died after being injected with a large air bubble.**

Her first victim, Liam Taylor, was admitted to the ward with a chest infection and placed in Allitt's care. After several incidents of his condition worsening then improving, the seven-week-old baby stopped breathing and went into cardiac arrest. The brain damage was so severe that the doctors were unable to resuscitate him. Allitt showed no emotion as she finished her shift and went home, returning to work the next day as if nothing had happened.

Over the next few months, children under Allitt's care continued to suffer unexplained cardiac arrests and apnoeic episodes, including a pair of two-month-old twins. One twin was killed with an insulin overdose, the other suffered permanent brain damage and paralysis due to overdoses of insulin and potassium. The twin's mother, who had befriended Allitt, actually made her the godmother of her surviving child.

No connection was made to Allitt until the death of her final victim, 15-month-old Claire Peck. The young girl was placed in Allitt's care following admittance for an asthma attack. She suffered two cardiac arrests while alone with Allitt, the second of which killed her. After Claire Peck's death, hospital staff became suspicious of the nurse and, following a brief investigation, discovered that Allitt was the only one on duty for all of the attacks and she had access to the drugs that could have caused these unexplained deaths.

While the true nature of her motives has never been fully explained, many detectives and psychiatrists believe that Allitt suffers from both Munchausen's and Munchausen's by Proxy syndrome. From a young age, Allitt would wear bandages and casts to draw attention to herself and, as she became older, she became aggressive and often complained of ailments that sent her to hospital. In one case, she even convinced a doctor to remove her healthy appendix then refused to let the wound heal by continually picking at the scar.

When she began working at a nursing home earlier in her career, she exhibited odd behaviour such as putting faeces on the walls and in the refrigerator. Doctors believe that when her actions failed to get her the attention she craved, her disorder shifted to Munchausen's by Proxy – injuring others in order to bring attention to herself.

She was convicted in May 1993 and is serving 13 concurrent life sentences in Rampton Secure Hospital in Nottinghamshire. After her arrest and imprisonment, Allitt began injuring herself – puncturing her breast to inject water, stabbing herself with paper-clips and burning herself with boiling water.

*ABOVE: Beverley Allitt is ushered into a police van following a court appearance*

# Joanna Dennehy

Joanna Dennehy is the third woman in the history of female killers to be given a whole-life prison term. Her notorious 'killing spree' took place in Peterborough in March 2013, where she attacked three victims, stabbing them to death.

- - - - - - - - - - - - - - - - - - - - - - - - - - - - - - - - - - - - - - - - - - - - - - - - - -

**On 29th March 2013, the body of property developer, Kevin Lee (one of Dennehy's ex-lovers), was discovered a day after his murder near Newborough. It was reported that the perpetrator dressed the victim in a black sequinned dress before dumping his body. The remaining two victims involved in the killing spree were Dennehy's housemates, Lukasz Slaboszewski and John Chapman. Slaboszewski was killed on 19th March and Chapman was murdered ten days later.**

*ABOVE: Dennehy took a grinning selfie photograph of herself as she searched out further victims*

The killer, Joanna Dennehy, was diagnosed with having multiple disorders; her psychiatrist claimed she possessed traits attributed to "psychopathic, anti-social and emotional instability". Dennehy admitted to her psychiatrist that she was "sadistic" and enjoyed stabbing men for entertainment. Public lawyer, Jenni Richards QC, described the killer as "arguably the most dangerous female prisoner in custody". Dennehy specifically targeted men on her killing spree.

During the multiple killings, Gary Richards and Leslie Layton assisted Dennehy on her spree. Both men stood trial and were charged with a range of crimes. In February 2014, Richards was found guilty of attempted murder and Layton was found guilty of perverting the course of justice. Dennehy had allegedly planned to kill nine men in total, aspiring to mimic the infamous killers Bonnie and Clyde.

In a documentary, which aired in January 2017, the killer's mother, Kathleen, described Dennehy as a being a "sensitive" and "polite" child. According to those who knew her, Dennehy's personality changed when she was in her mid-teens. She left home aged 16 and started drinking, taking drugs and dating a man named John Treanor, who is five years her senior. During a television interview, Kathleen spoke of her daughter's behaviour in court, saying "When I saw this footage of Jo, it was like somebody I didn't know ... that's not the kind, loving Jo that was our baby."

Dennehy was jailed in February 2014 after pleading guilty during her court appearance at the Old Bailey. She is one of just three women to be given a life sentence after admitting the murders of three victims. The other two confirmed cases are Myra Hindley and Rosemary West. Dennehy also pleaded guilty to two counts of attempted murder and preventing the lawful and decent burial of her victims.

In May 2016, a plot to kill or seriously harm a female security guard to escape from jail was leaked. Dennehy was the main culprit behind the plot, alongside two other inmates. Her plan of escape was found scrawled in the diary she kept in her cell. It was revealed that the plan involved murdering a guard, stealing her keys and cutting off her fingertips to bypass a biometric system.

Dennehy was placed in solitary confinement for two years. The killer was relocated to HMP Bronzefield near Ashford, Surrey. In response to these new conditions, the killer claimed her human rights had been violated and took her case to the high court. At London's High Court she claimed that she was being "unfairly and unlawfully" held in segregation at the facility. At a hearing in March, human rights lawyer, Hugh Southey QC, argued that Dennehy's incarceration and new conditions had left her "tearful and upset" and, at times, she had attempted to self-harm. The reputable lawyer described the perpetrator as being "vulnerable" due to her personality disorders and episodes of self-harming. However, government lawyers believed that the segregation was fair and ultimately justified.

*ABOVE: Serial killer, Joanna Dennehy, sticks out her tongue as she holds a jagged knife with handcuffs attached to her trousers*

# Dorothea Puente

An inveterate liar, Dorothea Puente's combination of deceit and greed would turn out to have deadly consequences.

- - - - - - - - - - - - - - - - - - - - - - - - - - - - - - - - - - - - - - - - - -

**Puente was born on 9ᵗʰ January 1929 and told friends that she was one of three children born and raised in Mexico. In reality, she was the daughter of cotton pickers who both died in the late 1930s, and raised by relatives in Fresno, California.**

*ABOVE: Dorothea Puente appears for arraignment in Sacramento, California Municipal Court in November 1988*

Puente suffered a turbulent personal life, much of it of her own making. She married four times, the first at the age of 16, but each ended in divorce as a result of her greed, promiscuity and lies. She had two daughters with her first husband and a third with another man, but never raised any of them. Two were given up for adoption and one was sent to live with relatives. She was arrested more times than she was married and, in the late 1940s, she began a habit of forging cheques as well as owning and managing a brothel in the 1960s.

After her fourth divorce, and having become addicted to easy money, Puente began hunting in bars for old men who were receiving benefits. She would pry them for information about their finances then forge their signatures to steal their benefits cheques. Although she was caught and convicted, she continued to commit the same crimes while on probation.

It was her acts in the 1980s, however, that revealed the depths she would go to for money. In 1980, she started renting a two-storey Victorian house at 1426 F Street in San Francisco, using it as a boarding house for the elderly and mentally ill. She ran a strict house, refusing her tenants use of the phone or allowing them to handle their own post. Puente stole their Social Security cheques and forged their signatures, but she then gave her clients a modest allowance while keeping the rest for herself. If her residents complained, they were literally buried in the backyard.

In the late 1980s, her neighbours began complaining about a horrible stench coming from Puente's property. She blamed various things, from the sewer being backed up to rats and fertiliser, as she spent her dead tenant's money on new clothes, expensive perfume and cosmetic surgery.

It was not until a social worker reported the disappearance of developmentally disabled schizophrenic Alvaro Montoya that the truth was uncovered. On 11th November 1988, while inquiring about Montoya, the police noticed disturbed soil on Puente's property. They discovered the body of Leona Carpenter, another of Puente's tenants. A search of the garden unearthed seven bodies, including Montayo, who was buried under an apricot tree, and Dorothy Miller, whose arms were duct taped to her chest. All were severely decomposed, while some were missing limbs or heads.

Puente was charged with nine murders. Although no cause of death could be determined in any of the cases, the prosecution argued that Puente subdued her victims with sleeping pills, suffocated them then hired convicts to bury the bodies.

Puente was convicted of three of the murders and sentenced to two life sentences. She maintained her innocence up to her death in  March 2011 at the age of 82, proclaiming every victim had died of natural causes.

*ABOVE: The boarding house where Dorothea Puente tried to cover the stench of dead bodies with air freshener*

# Aileen Wuornos

Aileen Wuornos never stood a chance of a normal life. Her father was a schizophrenic child molester who hanged himself in prison in 1969.

**Although Wuornos never knew her father, at three years old she was abandoned by her mother and raised by her abusive maternal grandparents. Her grandmother, an alcoholic, would beat her while her grandfather routinely sexually assaulted her. At just nine years old, she was engaging in sexual acts at school as well as with her brother.**

When Wuornos was 12 years old, she discovered that her grandparents were not her biological parents as she had been told and began acting up even more. At 14, she was raped by a friend of her grandfather's, became pregnant and gave birth to a son whom she gave up for adoption.

Soon after, her grandmother died and Wuornos left home. She supported herself through prostitution and hitch-hiking, and was in and out of prison in the 1970s and 1980s for various offences including assault and theft. After her grandfather committed suicide and her brother died of oesophageal cancer, Wuornos moved to Florida, where she would enact her own horrors.

After meeting her lesbian lover Tyria Moore in 1986, Wuornos supported them both as a truck-stop prostitute but this was also how she found her victims. She committed her first murder in December 1989. 51-year-old Richard Moore was a convicted rapist whose body, littered with bullet holes, was found miles from his abandoned car two weeks after his disappearance. Wuornos murdered a total of seven men between 1989-1990. Some were found clothed, some nude; all had been shot multiple times. The body of Peter Siems, victim number four, was never found. Moore never participated in any of the murders. Although she suspected what Wuornos was doing, and her lover even tried to describe her actions, Moore would tell her to stop as she didn't want to confront what was happening.

As the police noticed the similarities between the growing number of victims, the hunt for the murderer was on. When Wuornos and Moore were spotted abandoning Peter Siems's car, fingerprints found on it were matched to Wuornos. After a manhunt involving heavy surveillance and undercover police, Wuornos was arrested for outstanding warrants. With no evidence linking Wuornos to the murders, the police needed a confession. For this they turned to Moore, promising her immunity if she could secure Wuornos's confession. Moore made a series of taped calls to her lover; Wuornos suspected what Moore was doing and eventually gave her the confession she was seeking. She knew Moore was innocent and didn't want her to suffer for crimes she did not commit.

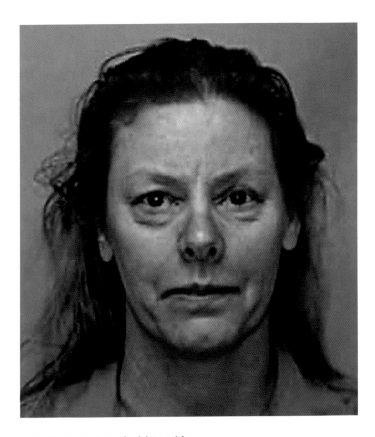

*ABOVE: Aileen Wuornos in an undated photograph from the Florida Department of Corrections*

Wuornos confessed to killing the men but said it was in self-defence, stating that each man had attempted to rape her. Her story, though, became inconsistent over time. She was convicted of murder and given six death sentences. After a last meal of a single cup of coffee, Wuornos was executed by lethal injection on 9th October 2002.

# Caroline Grills

Sixty-three year old mother, grandmother and great-grandmother Caroline Grills is one of history's most unlikely serial killers.

- - - - - - - - - - - - - - - - - - - - - - - - - - - - - - - - - - - - - - - - - - - - - - - - - - -

**A short, round woman with thick-rimmed glasses, Grills was known as Auntie Carrie to her extended family and often visited her relatives to bring them tea and cakes.**

Born around 1888 in Australia, Grills married and had five sons and a daughter. Two sons died in tragic circumstances, though this didn't seem to affect Auntie Carrie unduly. She was seen as loving and helpful by her family, always eager to prepare food and drinks but, in the late 1940s, many of her family members – mostly in-laws – began to feel ill, suffering from hair loss, progressive blindness and loss of speech. It wasn't until 1947, when illness became death, that the family became suspicious.

Christina Mickelson, Grills's 87-year-old stepmother, was the first to die in 1947. The following January, a relative of her husband's, 84-year-old Angelina Thomas, also died. The death of her husband's brother-in-law, John Lundberg, followed later in 1948, and Mary Anne Mickelson, a relative of her stepmother, died in 1949.

In late 1952, John Downey, another family member who had been suffering from occasional blindness, saw Auntie Carrie put something in his tea. Downey had already been admitted to hospital to be treated for thallium poisoning that April after eating preserved ginger given to him by Auntie Carrie. Between his previous poisoning, and having recently read a newspaper article on the recent outbreak of poisonings, he was already suspicious and quickly switched the cups. He took the confiscated tea to the police. Upon testing it, the police discovered it was indeed laced with thallium – an odourless and tasteless poison that, at the time, was used primarily as a rodent and ant poison.

When the police came to arrest Grills in 1953, they noticed she had Thal-Rat brand rat poison in her sideboard. They asked her why she kept it so near the food and she replied that she didn't think it would hurt. She then offered police chocolates which had been stored beside the poison, and they accepted the "treat" which were tested.

Grills was charged with four counts of murder and one count of attempted murder. While an exhumation of her previous victims proved that they had traces of thallium in their bodies, the murder charges were mainly circumstantial and were eventually dropped, leaving only of the charge of attempted murder. Although she professed her innocence in court, she exhibited odd behaviour such as occasionally bursting into laughter and her counsel had to warn her continuously not to laugh or smile during the trial. It took the jury just 12 minutes to convict her.

Grills was given the death penalty at first but that was later commuted to life in prison. She became affectionately known as "Aunt Thally" to her fellow inmates, and died in 1960 from peritonitis caused by a ruptured gastric ulcer. No motive was ever given for her crimes, making her case even more disturbing and mysterious.

*ABOVE: "Aunt Thally" would no doubt barely recognise the 21st Century Long Bay Correctional Centre where she spent the last seven years of her life*

# Mary Bell

Mary Bell's propensity for violence and murder in the 1960s made her one of Britain's most notorious child killers.

- - - - - - - - - - - - - - - - - - - - - - - - - - - - - - - - - - - - - - - - - - -

**Three-year-old Brian Howe lay dead amongst large concrete blocks in a derelict house in Scotswood, Newcastle upon Tyne. It was 31st July 1968 and his sister Pat was anxious to find her young, blond-haired brother who usually played close to home. His small body was discovered later that night by police.**

Mary Bell was born just 11 years before Brian's murder, to prostitute Betty Bell, who was habitually absent from home. Mary, or May as she was nicknamed, had been forced by her mother to commit sexual acts with men from a young age. She had also been subjected to several occasions where her mother had attempted to kill her and make the girl's death look accidental. While unsubstantiated, these vile acts on a young girl would undoubtedly lead to the deaths of two young boys by a child.

Martin Brown, aged four, was found strangled in a derelict house on 25th May 1968. Some days before, a three-year-old cousin of Bell's was found behind some empty sheds with a bleeding head. He was "found" by Mary Bell and her best friend, 13 year old, Norma Bell (no relation). It later transpired that Bell had pushed her cousin from a ledge. On 12th May 1968, Bell attacked three girls out playing. She placed her hands around the neck of two of the girls and squeezed hard. The police were called and the incident recorded, but Bell's violence was escalating and, 13 days later, Martin Brown was dead.

Martin was found at 3.30pm by three small boys. Shocked, they called out to construction workers nearby who had earlier given Martin some biscuits. The men desperately tried to revive the four year old, but he was already dead. At around the same time, Mary and Norma arrived at the derelict house and were told to go away. They went straight to Martin's aunt and told her that there had been an "accident" and there was "blood all over". An empty bottle of aspirin lay close to the dead child and there were no signs of violence. The official report at the time recorded the cause of death as "open". Meanwhile, the Bell girls questioned Martin's aunt about whether she missed the young boy, and whether she cried for him. June Brown, Martin's mother, received a chilling visit from Mary who wanted to see the dead boy in his coffin. Her request was refused and the front door shut firmly in her face.

Both Bell girls broke into a local nursery and left notes claiming to be the killers, but no one took any notice. Mary's taunting screams that she was a murderer also went unheeded as she was known to be a show-off.

Brian was also strangled, like Martin, but his thighs had been punctured and his genitals mutilated. He had been carved with an "N" that was changed to "M" on his stomach and, as far as police could tell, by a different hand. Police began to suspect the strange 11 year old who seemed excited by the murder. Bell was convicted of manslaughter on the grounds of diminished responsibility in December 1968. She was released 12 years later and, today, lives a life of anonymity.

*ABOVE: Mary Bell – a picture of innocence*

*RIGHT: Mary Bell escaped from prison in 1977, but was quickly recaptured*

# Jeanne Weber

Dubbed the "ogress" by French newspapers, Jeanne Weber was a child killer who strangled at least 10 children in the early 1900s in France, including three of her own.

**A stout woman with a round face, Weber moved to Paris when she was 14 years old, where she later married an alcoholic, gave birth to three children, and promptly became an alcoholic herself. Weber would babysit for friends or relatives, only to kill the children in her care.**

Though it's believed she caused the deaths of two of her own children prior to 1905, her killing spree began in March of that same year when she strangled to death her sister-in-law's 18-month-old daughter. The examining doctor ignored the bruises on the child's neck and believed Weber's claim that the child fell ill and died. Several days later, Weber was asked to babysit the woman's surviving daughter but, instead of the care she should have provided, Weber strangled the two-year-old girl. This time the doctor blamed the death on convulsions. Weber continued her pattern of murdering children, including her own son to allay suspicion, but every doctor who examined the corpses listed cause of death as an illness. It was not until Weber was caught attempting to strangle another sister-in-law's 10-year-old son that she was arrested and tried for multiple murders.

Miraculously, she was acquitted. The jury could not believe that a grieving mother could commit such atrocious acts. She was released back onto the streets and remained quiet for over a year, before turning up in a small French town under the name of Madame Moulinet. She summoned the local doctor to the house and showed him the nine-year-old boy she had been babysitting, who now lay dead in his bed. Despite the strange bruises on the boy's neck, the doctor listed the cause of death as convulsions. After Madame Moulinet was identified as Weber, he changed his original opinion. Again, Weber was tried and, again, she was released, when a second autopsy blamed the boy's death on typhoid.

After another disappearance, Weber resurfaced at a children's home when friends hired her to prove her innocence. Less than a week later, she was caught strangling one of the children, but the incident was covered up and Weber was quickly dismissed.

Weber then wandered France as a vagrant, staying out of the public eye until taking a room at an inn in Commercy in May 1908. Stating she was scared of sleeping alone, she convinced the innkeepers to allow their seven year old son to sleep with her. Around 11.00pm that night, the woman next door heard strange sobs and screams. When she and the innkeepers went into Weber's room, they found the boy dead with his eyes bulging and blood down his nightshirt. He had bitten his tongue, while Weber lay asleep with her arm around the corpse and blood on her nightgown. This time, Weber could not escape imprisonment.

During her trial, she was declared insane and sent to an asylum in Mareville, France. She remained there until she committed suicide two years later.

*ABOVE: The front page of French newspaper "Le Petit Journal" on 12th May 1907 with Jeanne Weber accused of infanticide for a second time*

# Belle Gunness

Notorious black widow Belle Gunness was born in Norway around 1859, but no one knows exactly when or how she died.

----

**She was an exceptionally large woman, standing over 1.8 metres tall and weighing over 14 stone. Legend has it that a pregnant Gunness was in her native Norway one night when a wealthy man kicked her in the stomach, causing her to miscarry. The man was never prosecuted and Gunness's personality drastically changed.**

She emigrated to the United States in 1881 to seek her fortune, which she would find at the deaths of many others. After working as a servant for several years, she married her first husband in 1884 and had four children. Two of the children died of mysterious causes, and her husband died in 1900 after suffering symptoms of strychnine poisoning. After her husband's death, Gunness collected enough money from the insurance company to buy a farm in Indiana. This farm became a death trap for lonely, wealthy men.

Gunness married again in April 1902, to Peter Gunness, and tragedy followed shortly thereafter. His infant daughter died one week later while alone in Gunness' care and Peter, himself, would die in December of that year. Gunness said it was an accident and collected the insurance money, but the case was declared murder and brought before a coroner's jury. Somehow, Gunness was able to convince the jury of her innocence.

It was in 1907 that Gunness systematically began murdering wealthy, single men. She hired farmhand Ray Lamphere to help her run the farm, and cover up her murders, while she placed advertisements in the matrimonial columns of various newspapers. She would write to the men, invite them to the farm and murder them after they arrived. Lamphere later confessed that Gunness used various methods to dispose of her suitors. She would drug their coffee and bash in their heads with a meat grinder or smother them in chloroform while they slept. Once dead, she would take them to the cellar where she butchered them, either burying the remains or, if she was tired, feeding them to the hogs.

Gunness eventually fired Lamphere, tired of his infatuation with her, but he continued to harass her so she made plans for her own escape. She made false reports to the police that Lamphere threatened to burn down her farm, setting the stage for her own arson.

On 28th April 1908, as Gunness's farmhouse burned, four bodies were discovered inside – three children and one decapitated woman. While the woman was originally believed to be Gunness, it was determined that the body was too small. Later, it was discovered that the unidentified woman had been poisoned with strychnine. Dozens of human remains were found as police excavated the property and it is believed she killed anywhere between 20 or 40 people, possibly more.

*ABOVE: Belle Gunness with her children Lucy Sorensen, Myrtle Sorensen and Philip Gunness in 1904*

Although Gunness's distinctive dental work was found in the ashes, it has never been determined if she perished in the fire or not. Unconfirmed sightings of her were reported across the United States right up until the 1930s.

ABOVE: A search is carried out on Saddleworth Moor for
missing children Keith Bennett, Pauline Reade and John
Kilbride in October 1965. All three were the victims of
Moors Murderers Ian Brady and Myra Hindley

# Multiple Killers

# John Allen Muhammad and Lee Boyd Malvo

The Beltway Sniper Attacks took place in Virginia, Maryland and Washington D.C. over the duration of three weeks in October 2002.

---

**The attacks resulted in the confirmed deaths of 10 civilians going about their daily business and the critical injury of three others. Because of the closeness in time between murder locations, it was believed that the perpetrator was using Interstate 495 (also known as the Capital Beltway), to move between states.**

John Allen Williams (later changed to Muhammad) was the triggerman and mastermind behind the attacks. His accomplice, Lee Boyd Malvo, a minor at the time, was convinced by the older man that their actions would result in a sanctuary being built for homeless, black children. Williams had been exposed to military training while serving seven years in the Louisiana Army National Guard. He was commended for his ability with a rifle after receiving the expert rifleman's badge and advanced to the rank of sergeant. In 1971, he joined the Nation of Islam and, in 2001, legally changed his surname to Muhammad.

*ABOVE: The weapon used in the sniper shootings is displayed during opening arguments of the trial*

*ABOVE: Lee Boyd Malvo walks out of the Fairfax County Juvenile Court House*

Muhammad met Malvo in Antigua around 1999, where the pair then became closely acquainted. Muhammad schemed a plan that aimed to terrorise the US government, and would result in a large sum of money being paid out to the pair. The plan consisted of three phases; phase one was to shoot six white people per day for a month. Phase two was to shoot a pregnant woman in the stomach and a police officer. Phase three would consist of attending the police officer's funeral, at which they would let off explosives hoping to kill many more police officers and ambulance crews. Phase one did not go as planned, and the pair were caught before they managed to implement phase two.

*ABOVE: Sniper suspect John Allen Muhammad handles a rifle scope during cross examination of Sgt. Maj. Mark Spicer during his trial*

The deathly duo travelled around in a blue Chevrolet Caprice, where Muhammad had cut a sniper hole into the rear of the vehicle, allowing a clear shot to be made without even leaving the car. By using the same vehicle, the killers were easily identifiable. After police put out a description of the vehicle they were looking for, they received a tip off that it was parked at a rest stop just off Interstate 70 near Maryland. The car was immediately surrounded by police and the two men were found sleeping inside it next to the murder weapon (a Bushmaster XM-15 rifle). At their trial, Muhammad was given the death penalty and Malvo was imprisoned for life. On 10th November 2009, Muhammad was executed by lethal injection and Malvo is currently still serving life.

# Marc Dutroux and Michelle Martin

Belgian serial killer Marc Dutroux was convicted of the kidnap, torture, sexual abuse and murder of four girls between 1995 and 1996.

**Two other girls were also subjected to his depraved behaviour, although they survived their attacks. All Dutroux's victims were aged between 8 and 19 years old.**

Dutroux's two marriages, which resulted in five children, both ended in divorce, due to the unemployed electrician's long criminal history, which included drug dealing, violent crime and stolen vehicles. Dutroux worked with a number of accomplices including his second wife, Michelle Martin, Bernard Weinstein – who he was later accused of murdering – and drug addict Michel Lelièvre. The sexually motivated crimes, however, dated back to February 1986 when he was arrested alongside Martin for the abduction and rape of five

young girls. Martin received five years in prison (during which time she married Dutroux), and he received more than 13 years, although was released for good behaviour in 1992 (having served just three years). His own mother wrote to the parole board to express her concerns that she believed her son was keeping girls captive in one of his seven houses, but her letters were essentially ignored.

As soon as Dutroux was released from prison a campaign of terror towards children began and he even persuaded a psychiatrist to prescribe him with sedatives, which he later used to subdue his victims, as well as to write a report into his psychiatric state, which led to him gaining a government pension.

Mèlissa Russo, aged eight, and Julie Lejeune, also eight, were kidnapped by Dutroux on 24th June 1995. Both girls were repeatedly sexually assaulted and forced to take part in pornographic videos. Two months later, he abducted two teenagers camping in Ostend. An Marchal, 17, and 19-year-old Eefje Lambrecks were chained to a bed in Dutroux's house, because his specially built cellar room already housed the two younger children. Several weeks later, the two older girls were sedated before being buried alive at one of Dutroux's other properties.

Dutroux was arrested and held in custody for three months on car-related crimes between 1995 and 1996, but even a search of his home, where Mèlissa and Julie's cries could be heard by police, failed to secure their safety. Martin, claiming she was too afraid to go into the basement, did not feed the children and they eventually starved to death. They were buried in the back garden of one of Dutroux's houses.

Following his release in 1996, he kidnapped Sabine Dardenne, 12, whom he also kept in the basement. However, it was his kidnap of 14-year-old Laetitia Delhez, three months later in August 1996, that led to his arrest. A vigilant resident spotted Laetitia's abduction and was able to give a good description of Dutroux's van and part of the number plate. He, his wife and Lelièvre were arrested. Two days later, the terrified victims were found alive in the basement of the killer's house by police. It took seven years for Dutroux's case to be tried. He is held in solitary confinement serving life. Martin received 30 years.

*ABOVE: Marc Dutroux sits in the dock of the courthouse in the southeastern Belgian town of Arlon*

*OPPOSITE: Shelves hid a cache in the house in Marcinelle, a suburb of the Belgian southern city of Charleroi, where Marc Dutroux incarcerated and abused his young victims*

# Michel Fourniret and Monique Olivier

French carpenter Michel Fourniret came to public attention in 2004, just as the case against serial killer Marc Dutroux was coming to an end.

**After hearing that Dutroux's wife, Michelle Martin, had received 30 years for her part in helping her husband get away with murder, Monique Olivier approached police to let them know that her own husband, a known paedophile, had murdered nine people. Not all his victims were children.**

ABOVE: Michel Fourniret (second right) pictured at his arrival in Liege's court house

Fourniret was already serving time in a Belgian prison for trying to abduct a 13-year-old girl when he confessed to the murders of six victims whose ages ranged from 12 to 22, although he denied three other murders of which his wife said he was responsible, including the couple's 16-year-old Belgian au pair.

Olivier was aware that her husband went "hunting" for new victims. He would lure young girls and women into his vehicle before raping them and later murdering them. Olivier was also used by her husband to help put victims at their ease by being in the couple's car when the girls were lured from safety, and she was later arrested and charged with failing to help any of them, and for aiding in their kidnappings. Two months later, Fourniret admitted to killing two further victims identified by his wife, but continued to refuse to admit any part in the death of the couple's au pair. He was also accused of 10 further murders and eventually found guilty of seven of them.

His first arrest came in 1966 when he molested a child. His first wife divorced him and he remarried. His second wife, who bore him three children, also divorced him when he was again arrested and convicted of the rape of a number of children. He met Monique Olivier through an advert he placed looking for a pen pal. Fourniret promised to kill Olivier's abusive husband if she promised to help him look for virgins. Two months after he left prison, in 1987, the two travelled around looking for victims and the killing spree began.

In December 1987, 17-year-old Isabelle Laville became their first victim. It took the Belgian and French police many years to work out they were looking for a serial killer in the Ardennes area and, for a long time, no one connected any of Fourniret's crimes.

Known as the "Beast of Ardennes", Fourniret was sentenced to life imprisonment in 2008 with no hope of parole for at least 22 years. Olivier was given a life sentence for complicity and ordered to serve a minimum of 28 years.

*LEFT: A bunch of flowers is laid at the site where the body of French woman Jeanne-Marie Desramault was dug up by police with the help of Fourniret in July 2004 at a chateau in the town of Donchery*

*BELOW: The Chateau de Sautou estate in Donchery, French Ardennes, where forestry worker Michel Fourniret confessed to murdering six girls whose bodies were reported to be buried close to the premises*

# Paul Bernardo and Karla Homolka

In 1990, when she became engaged to Paul Bernardo, Karla Homolka could not have been happier.

- - - - - - - - - - - - - - - - - - - - - - - - - - - - - - - - - - - - - - - - - - - - - - - -

**She had a wonderful man to call her own and a lavish wedding to look forward to. She would have done anything to keep her new fiancé happy – and she did.**

*ABOVE: Paul Bernardo (right) on his way to a pre-trial hearing with a member of the Toronto Police*

Bernardo was dissatisfied that Homolka was not a virgin when they met and he told her that it was her duty to provide him with one to satisfy his needs. He decided that the virgin in question should be Homolka's pretty younger sister, Tammy, with whom he regularly flirted. He wanted to have sex with the 15-year-old without her knowledge or consent. Once Homolka was convinced that she should "give" her sister to Bernardo, it was just a question of logistics.

Homolka stole an anaesthetic that animals inhale before surgery from the veterinary practice where she worked and, on Christmas Eve 1990, the couple plied Tammy with alcohol and the sedative Halcion. As Homolka's family drifted off to bed at their home in St Catherines, Ontario, Tammy lay on the couch dozing. Bernardo videoed himself raping Tammy. He then ordered Homolka to make sexual advances to her sister, but Tammy suddenly woke up and vomited. Homolka tried to clear her sister's mouth and throat but, tragically, the girl died choking on her own vomit. Homolka called the emergency services and Tammy's death was treated as accidental.

Bernardo wasn't satisfied that his "Christmas present" had died during his fantasy and demanded that Homolka provide him with another "gift". Leslie Mahaffey became the couple's next victim in June 1991. Like Tammy, Leslie was plied with alcohol and Halcion before being subjected to 24 hours of rape and abuse at the hands of both captors. By this time, police had already built a profile of Bernardo – who had committed a series of rapes and who was known as the "Scarborough Rapist". (Once his photo was officially released, many former colleagues and friends phoned police pointing the finger at Bernardo.) In fact, Homolka had encouraged and even videoed some of his attacks on women. One victim remembered a woman being present during her attack, but the police initially dismissed the idea as hysteria. They couldn't have been more wrong. Homolka was explicitly involved in the rapes and abuse of young women. Leslie was strangled and dismembered by the couple before being found encased in cement in Lake Gibson at the end of June 1991. She was 14 years old.

ABOVE: The carriage that was used to ferry
Karla Homolka and Paul Bernardo from their wedding
in Niagara on the Lake. The carriage has been stored
in a barn in the town since its notoriety grew
during the trial

ABOVE: An artist's impression of Karla Homolka as she
appeared in court in Joliette, Quebec, June 2005

On 16th April 1992, 15-year-old Kristen French became the couple's
third kidnap victim when she was forced into their car at knifepoint
and held captive for three days. The young girl was tortured, and
forced to drink large quantities of alcohol while the couple videoed
their atrocities. On 19th April, Kristen was murdered and her
naked body was found later that month dumped in a ditch.

By 1993, DNA samples proved Bernardo to be the rapist the
police had been seeking. Tammy's body was exhumed and
Bernardo was convicted in September 1995 of two first-degree
murders, two aggravated sexual assaults and other offences.
He was sentenced to life imprisonment. Homolka was also sent
to prison, but released in 2005 having agreed a plea bargain
and given testimony against Bernardo.

# Francis Heaulme and accomplices

A childhood of abuse and torture moulded Francis Heaulme into "The Criminal Backpacker".

---

**Heaulme's father, a gambler and alcoholic, beat and abused his son severely until he reached 17 years old. The torture would include being suspended by his wrists from a wire in the cellar if he failed to bring his father bottles of alcohol.**

As a teenager, Heaulme – born in Metz, France, in 1959 – also became an alcoholic, and gashed himself on the arms, legs and chest with glass from broken bottles. Despite the horrors he endured at the hands of his father, Heaulme loved his sister Christine and idolised his mother Nicole, who died of cancer when he was 23. Heaulme was absolutely distraught.

He threw himself upon the lid of her coffin, in the grave, and declared that he wished to be buried with her before later making several failed suicide attempts. On the day his mother died, a child known as "Little Grégory" disappeared and Heaulme became morbidly obsessed with the case, avidly collecting newspaper reports of the abduction.

*ABOVE: Francis Heaulme (centre) in October 2006 in Montigny-les-Metz during a re-enactment near railroad tracks where two children, Alexandre Beckrich and Cyril Beyning, were found dead in September 1986*

Heaulme left his family following his mother's death to travel around France. Described as a "vagabond alcoholic", he hitchhiked and travelled on trains, although he was rarely in possession of a valid ticket. He found shelter through the Emmaus charity, with its psychiatric hospitals and hostels for alcoholics. He took occasional work as an itinerant stonemason and metalworker, but he spent his wages on drink and tranquillizers, often mixing the two.

Between 1984 and 1992, the French police had been hunting a serial killer who was leaving a trail of stabbed or strangled corpses strewn across France. On 7th January 1992, Heaulme was arrested at Bischerwiller in Alsace. He was charged with the murder of Aline Peres in Brest in 1988, a vicious killing that was perpetrated on a crowded public beach, surrounded by witnesses who saw nothing.

Detectives throughout France interviewed Heaulme about unsolved murder cases that shared similarities with the murderer's supposed modus operandi. However, Heaulme proved very difficult to question. According to Jean-François Abgrall, who arrested Heaulme: "He doesn't lie. He never makes anything up. But he deliberately covers his tracks by mixing the crimes, dates and locations", and: "It's when you ask him nothing that he says the most."

It transpired that Heaulme had two accomplices in the rapes and serial murders, Joseph Molins and Didier Gentil. Heaulme suffered from Klinesfelter's syndrome, rendering him unable to commit sexual assaults himself, therefore Heaulme's accomplices undertook the rapes while Heaulme watched, then he murdered the victims by strangulation, stabbing or slitting their throats.

Because of the torturous and confused nature of the case, which embraced many brutal killings that had been committed across the country, it took two trials to convict Heaulme. In May 1997, he was tried for several murders at the Court of Var. He was sentenced to life in prison, with no chance of parole for 22 years. On 16th December 2004, Heaulme was sentenced to a further 30 years with no chance of parole for 20, for three murders he had committed in the Marne area in 1988 and 1989.

*BELOW: Francis Heaulme at Metz Courthouse in August 1993*

# Adolfo Constanzo and followers

Adolfo de Jesus Constanzo began an apprenticeship with a Haitian priest in order to learn the skills to "profit from evil".

It was the 1970s and Constanzo, also known as "El Padrino de Matamoros", was in his teens and free to worship his chosen faith. His mother had her six-month-old son blessed by a Haitian priest who practised "palo mayombe", where a liquid prepared by boiling human bones in it was drunk. The family's beliefs were kept secret, but he and his mother often travelled to Haiti or San Juan for his religious "education".

In 1972, the family returned to Miami, where Constanzo had been born, following the death of his stepfather. His mother remarried a man involved in the drugs trade and the occult, but Constanzo was about to establish his own cult and by 1976 believed that he had developed psychic powers. Also believing that he had great abilities, he committed himself to Kadiempembe, his faith's version of Satan in 1983, and soon made his way to Mexico City to recruit his first disciples. He seduced Martin Quintana Rodriguez and Omar Orea Ochoa and moved in with them before offering his abilities in fortune telling and ritual cleansing to the wider community.

News of Constanzo began to spread and he used his "premonitions" to aid drug dealers scheduling their shipments and other illegal activities. Within three years, he amassed a considerable fortune and was able to boast of crime bosses, high profile drug cartels and senior law enforcement officials amongst his clientele.

*BELOW: The former home of drug dealer and leader of satanic cult Adolfo de Jesus Constanzo, which neighbours claim is hexed*

As a teenager, under an "apprenticeship", Constanzo had often robbed local graves of bones for his teacher's cauldron. While in Mexico City, Constanzo's own cauldron was used for many human offerings and it is cited that he and his cult were responsible for 23 ritual murders in the area. At the end of April 1987, Constanzo became incensed when the Calzada crime family refused him full membership to their syndicate. Seven members of the family were tortured and mutilated and fed into Constanzo's cauldron, but police were unable to connect him to the murders.

The deaths, and the fact he evaded police, convinced Constanzo of his special powers and he moved his cult to a ranch where killings began in earnest. Constanzo would seek victims immediately after a ritual human sacrifice. While the deaths of drug dealers, crime families and locals were investigated by police, their powers were fairly limited and efforts to bring the serial killer to justice failed. However, when

*ABOVE: Portrait of drug and voodoo mass murders leader Adolfo de Jesus Constanzo*

Constanzo commanded his cult to bring him an American student for sacrifice, it would prove his undoing. The cult murdered young American Mark Kilroy and the wealthy man's family put immense pressure on both the United States and South American authorities to help find him.

During April and May 1989, the cult members, having fled the ranch, were picked up one by one. Constanzo was hiding out, but police stumbled across him in an apartment while investigating another case. In panic, Constanzo began shooting at police. The shootout lasted 45 minutes but, knowing there was no escape, Constanzo ordered another cult member to shoot him and his lover, Martin Quintana. He was dead by the time police stormed the building.

# Andras Pandy and Agnes Pandy

By the end of the 1990s, the authorities faced increasing criticism and pressure from the Belgian people to put an end to a recent spate of kidnappings, disappearances and murders.

**Public anger was rife and investigators, desperately hoping to be shown some faith, began pouring over old cases where they discovered the bizarre statements and interviews from Agnes Pandy, made in 1993, about her father's alleged crimes.**

*ABOVE: Andras Pandy and his daughter Agnes*

*OPPOSITE: Hungarian-born pastor and former teacher of protestant religion Andras Pandy arrives at the Brussels court house in February 2002, where he was on trial for allegedly murdering six members of his family and possibly eight other people*

Andras Pandy, a protestant minister, had been raping his then 38-year-old daughter since she was 13. His control over Agnes was total, vicious and extreme, and would lead the non-descript young woman into a life of violence, abuse and ultimately murder. Andras was undoubtedly the dominant partner in the relationship and turned his daughter into his sex slave before he sent her and her older brother on holiday to the Belgian coast in 1993. When they returned, her stepmother, Edith Pandy, and her younger sister, Andrea, were missing, but her father told her not to look for them as they would not be returning home. Agnes nevertheless went to the police, who questioned Pandy, but there was no evidence to suggest anything was amiss and certainly no proof that Agnes had been sexually assaulted. During questioning by police, Pandy claimed that his daughter and wife had returned to their native Hungary and produced letters in evidence to back up his explanation. As a minister, Pandy was a part of Belgian society that was trusted, and it was a time before the Detroux affair had yet to be unearthed. Therefore the case was closed.

However, in 1997, the Pandy case was revisited and the shocking truth unravelled. Having brutalised his daughter over many years, Pandy turned his daughter into his accomplice and Agnes helped him to kill and dispose of five of the six victims that she eventually spoke to police about. The six people he had killed included his first two wives and four of his children and stepchildren. When police first investigated the deaths at Pandy's "House of Horrors", as it was dubbed by the press, they discovered that the sets of teeth and body parts they found in the house were actually from other people.

Agnes described to investigators how a number of the victims were shot, while Pandy bludgeoned others to death with a sledgehammer. Once dead, all victims were hacked to pieces by both father and daughter in order to dispose of their corpses. Some were wrapped in plastic, while others were dumped in an acidic drain cleaner until their flesh and bones had disappeared completely.

The incestuous minister was found guilty on six counts of murder, three counts of rape and sentenced to life imprisonment, while Agnes Pandy was sentenced to 21 years on five counts of murder. Andras Pandy died on 23rd December 2016.

# David and Catherine Birnie

David and Catherine Birnie first met in a Perth suburb in Western Australia when they were 12 years old and began dating two years later.

**David came from a home shrouded in neglect and abuse while motherless Catherine endured a bitter custody dispute between her father and maternal grandparents. The teens were often in trouble with the police and Catherine's family urged her to sever ties with the boy, believing the relationship could only lead to grief. They had no idea, however, that it would lead to murder.**

The pair separated during their teens for a number of years when David left school to be an apprentice jockey, and Catherine spent time in prison. David was often caught abusing the horses and once tried to rape an elderly woman. They both married other people, but the couple reconnected after the birth of Catherine's seventh child when David tracked her down in hospital and she abandoned her husband.

In their house on Moorhouse Street, David and Catherine often fantasised about raping and murdering women. These fantasies became a reality on 6th October 1986 when they abducted a woman who had come to their house to buy tyres. Mary Neilson, a 22-year-old student, was chained to the Birnies' bed then raped by David while Catherine stood by. They then drove her to Gleneagles National Park where they raped her again and strangled her to death. While Mary's murder was unplanned, it started a month-long killing spree that would result in the abduction and torture of four more young girls.

Only two weeks after the murder, they kidnapped hitchhiking teenager Susannah Candy. Like Mary, Candy was tied up and raped by David while Catherine watched. This time, though, it was Catherine who strangled her. They buried Susannah near Mary in Gleneagles and, on 1st November, found their next victim. Thirty-one year old Noelene Patterson was abused just like the others but, this time, David became attached to his victim and kept her alive for three days. Jealous of the situation, Catherine finally ordered that David kill her. He forced Noelene to take sleeping pills then strangled her while she slept and her body was buried close to the others.

The next day, 21-year-old Denise Brown was taken from a bus stop and forced at knifepoint to go to the Moorhouse Street address where her death would be the most brutal. After chaining her and raping her at the house, the Birnies took her to the park and raped her again, David stabbing her in the neck as he did so. As they started to bury Brown, she sat up in her grave so David struck her in the head twice with an axe, finally killing her. Several days later, the Birnies kidnapped their final victim, but the 17-year-old managed to escape and run to the police. The Birnies were apprehended and confessed after a long interrogation. Each was found guilty of four counts of murder. David hanged himself in prison in 2005 while Catherine is currently serving four consecutive life sentences.

*ABOVE: Catherine Birnie is escorted by policewomen*

*ABOVE: The shallow grave of one of David and Catherine Birnie's victims in Gleneagle Forest*

*LEFT: The Birnies's home on Moorhouse Street*

# Fred and Rosemary West

A vicious and sexually exploitative couple, Fred and his wife, Rosemary 'Rose' West, murdered at least 11 girls between 1967 and 1987.

**Each victim was held captive in the Wests' house, sexually abused and tortured for several days before being murdered, dismembered and buried in the garden, cellar or on one of Fred's construction sites. Many victims were young women they hunted at bus stops. Some were the Wests's own daughters.**

Both Fred and Rose West were raised in sexually abusive homes. Fred's father had incestuous relationships with his daughters and taught his young son that incest was normal. As a child, Rose was repeatedly raped by her own father. Their incestuous relationship continued, with her husband's blessing, after Rose's marriage to Fred.

Prior to meeting Rose, Fred married Rena Costello, who gave birth to a daughter, Charmaine, in 1963. Both Rena and Charmaine would become victims of the Wests. While still married to Rena, Fred met Rose and the two began dating. Rose moved in with Fred when she was 16 and gave birth to their first daughter, Heather Ann, though it's suspected that Heather Ann was a result of Rose's incestuous relationship with her father. Possessive of her new relationship, Rose murdered Charmaine in June 1971 while Fred was serving a prison sentence for theft. When Rena came to look for her daughter, Fred murdered her to avoid questions about Charmaine.

After Fred and Rose married in January 1972, Fred encouraged his wife into prostitution, going so far as to set up a special room in their house where she could meet clients that included peepholes so he could watch through the door. Rose gave birth to a total of seven children, three of whom were mixed race – a result of her prostitution. One of these daughters, Anna Marie, was eight years old when Fred West bound and gagged her in the cellar then raped her while her mother watched. Anna Marie was the focus of her father's attacks for many years until she finally left home. Fred then focused his rage on Heather Ann, who was less fortunate than her sister. After Heather told a school friend about her father's activities, Fred murdered her, dismembered her, and buried her in the garden with his son's enforced help.

The Wests' decades of murder and abuse came to an end when another young victim confided in a friend who then told the police. The police arrested the Wests in 1992 after discovering vast amounts of pornography and evidence of child abuse in their home. When the surviving West children told the police how their father warned them to be good or they would "end up under the porch like Heather", the police made the gruesome discoveries of multiple bodies in the garden and cellar.

Fred West hanged himself in prison before he could be tried for his crimes. Rose was convicted of 10 murders and condemned to die in prison. Unlike Fred, she has never admitted to any of the crimes.

*ABOVE: A police officer stands guard outside the Wests's home at 25 Cromwell Street, Gloucester*

*OPPOSITE: Team members remove evidence from Cromwell Street*

# Giancarlo Lotti and Mario Vanni

Florence, Italy, was the setting between 1968 and 1985 for a series of 16 murders, where nearly all the victims were couples.

**Following a trip to the cinema in August 1968, six-year-old Natalino Mele was asleep on the back seat of the car in which his mother, Barbara Locci, and her lover, Antonio Lo Bianco, were enjoying sexual intercourse. They were shot dead in the cemetery where they were parked by an unknown assailant.**

The child was either taken by the killer out of the car and left on the doorstep of a nearby house at 2.00am in the morning, or he found his way there by himself. Natalino was so traumatised by the incident, even he didn't know how he got there. Locci, known as "Queen Bee" for her extra-marital relationships, was the first victim in a series of cold-blooded murders that would span almost two decades. Stefano Mele, Locci's husband, was the first suspect to be arrested but, while he was known to be fed up with his wife's infidelities and even confessed to the killings, he failed to mention his son during the murders or what had happened to him. He subsequently changed his story and claimed that an accomplice, Salvatore Vinci, was responsible. Mele was eventually convicted of the killings and sentenced to 14 years in prison but, in 1974, two more bodies were found in a car, shot by a .22 Beretta, the same weapon used in the first two murders.

One of the victims, 18-year-old Stefania Pettini, was found posed by the killer in a spread-eagled position where her vagina had been mutilated by a vine branch. Her boyfriend, 19-year-old Pasquale Gentilcore, was found naked at the rear of the vehicle. Stefania had been stabbed at least 96 times in a frenzied attack. Three men were quickly arrested, but later released without charge. What was clear was that police were looking for a sexual deviant and Mele was obviously not responsible for the first two murders.

Seven years later in June 1981, two lovers were shot dead with the same .22 Beretta. Carmela De Nuccio, 21, was found at the bottom of a steep bank close to the parked car where the body of her boyfriend, Giovanni Fogg, was found slumped over the steering wheel. Her vagina had been surgically removed. Four months later, another couple was killed in the vicinity. The 24-year-old's vagina was also removed, but a larger area of flesh had been taken and her abdomen split by a seven-inch, single-blade knife. A sadistic serial killer was cold-bloodedly preying on young couples. When a fourth couple was killed in June 1982, police believed the killer had been disturbed before he could mutilate his female victim. More victims followed before the deaths of a young couple in woodland near Vicchio di Mugello. The female victim's vagina was removed, as was her left breast and she was slashed with a knife more than 100 times. The killer, by now known as the "Monster of Florence", sent a portion of the left breast of another victim, Nadine Mauriot, along with a note to the state prosecutor to say that two more murders had occurred.

ABOVE: Giancarlo Lotti

*ABOVE: Mario Vanni*

Convicted sex offender Pietro Pacciani was charged with the murders but the conviction was ruled unsafe by the Court of Appeal in 1994. That same year, Pacciani's associates Giancarlo Lotti and Mario Vanni stood trial for five of the double murders following a confession by Lotti. They were sentenced to life imprisonment. However, police still strongly believe that a much larger group of sadistic men, all members of a cult, were responsible for the deaths of the couples and that the "Monster of Florence" was never fully brought to justice.

# Charles Manson and followers

Charles Manson's taste for crime began at a young age with burglary and he spent time in and out of juvenile prisons, where he often managed to escape.

- - - - - - - - - - - - - - - - - - - - - - - - - - - - - - - - - - - - - - - - - -

**In 1961, when Manson was held at the United States Penitentiary serving an adult sentence, he met a prisoner named Alvin Karpis (of the Barker-Karpis gang) who taught him to play the guitar. Soon Manson became obsessed with music and songwriting and believed that, upon his release, he would become a world famous musician.**

After being released from his second long-term imprisonment on 21st March 1967, Manson – born on 12th November 1934 in Cincinnati, Ohio – attempted to pursue his music career, while being introduced to the likes of record producer Terry Melcher and Dennis Wilson of The Beach Boys. Manson's obsession led to him traveling the United States and, with his popular songs and characteristic personality, he managed to develop a small following which he named "The Family". The Family followed him everywhere and eventually moved in with

*ABOVE: Charles Manson*

Manson in the famous Spahn Movie Ranch. From here, Manson proceeded to develop his very own religious beliefs for the family to follow, which appeared to have borrowed the moralistic philosophy associated with the Process Church, widely known for its Satan worship.

Becoming further obsessed with music, Manson took a shine to The Beatles's song "Helter Skelter", which he believed was lyrically about the race war between black and white people and how the black people were going to rise up against the white race. Manson thought he could "show the blacks how it was done" by starting an uprising of his own. The perfect opportunity arose when his music career began to run stale. Obsessed, deranged, completely deluded and failing, he blamed those who had previously guided him musically, for his inability to become famous.

In 1969, Manson sent four "family" members to a specific address in Los Angeles where Terry Melcher had once resided. The family members brutally murdered a woman who was carrying an unborn child and four other people that were residing at the address. Little did Manson know that Melcher had left the property some time before and that he had just ordered the murder of eight-and-a-half-month pregnant actress Sharon Tate who was the wife of movie director Roman Polanski.

The following night, the family struck again at a separate address accompanied by Manson himself. After the cult members gained access to the property, both Leno and Rosemary LaBianca were stabbed numerous times with a bayonet, while pillowcases covered their heads. The murder was traced back to Manson and his cronies and, on 25th January 1971, he was found guilty of first-degree murder and conspiracy to commit murder.

Manson was originally sentenced to death but was pardoned from execution in 1972 when Californian law outlawed the death penalty. Today, he continues to serve his life imprisonment in California's Corcoran Prison.

*OPPOSITE: Charles Manson's "family" hold vigil near the courthouse during the Sharon Tate murder trial*

# Ian Brady and Myra Hindley

Described as a 'sexually sadistic psychopath', Ian Brady and his accomplice Myra Hindley carried out the notorious Moors Murders that horrified the nation.

**The couple were responsible for the sexual torture and deaths of five children, aged between 10 and 17, during the early to mid-1960s in and around Greater Manchester.**

Despite their trial for five murders in 1966, the real extent of Brady and Hindley's crimes did not come to light until 1985 and both maintained their innocence until this time.

Pauline Reade disappeared on her way to a dance on 12th July 1963. The young girl was 16 years old and a friend of Hindley's younger sister Maureen. She was offered a lift by Hindley, at Brady's request, who asked Pauline to help her search for a lost glove on Saddleworth Moor. Brady followed the van driven by Hindley onto the moor on his motorbike. He then took Pauline to look for the glove while Hindley waited at the van. Thirty minutes later he returned alone.

He sexually assaulted Pauline before slitting her throat and leaving her to die. Brady and Hindley then buried her on the moor before putting the motorbike in the back of the van and driving home. The couple abducted 12-year-old John Kilbride on 23rd November that same year. He was also taken to the moor on the pretext of looking for a lost glove. Brady sexually assaulted the boy before trying to slit his throat. The killer eventually strangled him with a piece of rope.

Six months later, on 16th June 1964, four days after his 12th birthday, Keith Bennett vanished on the way to his grandmother's house. Keith had been driven to Saddleworth Moor, also to look for a missing glove. Brady sexually assaulted him before strangling him with rope.

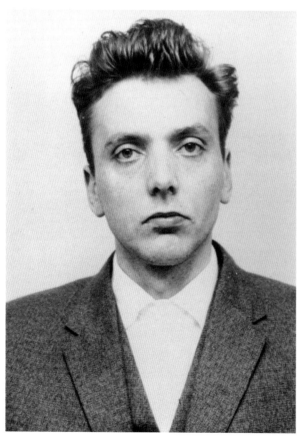

*ABOVE: Ian Brady*

*ABOVE: Myra Hindley*

*ABOVE: A police search team looks for the body of Keith Bennett. Operation Maida was launched in 2003 as a new attempt to locate his body, but was called off in 2009 with Greater Manchester Police having exhausted all of the avenues available to them*

Lesley Ann Downey was just 10 years old when she was lured away from a fairground in December 1964 by Brady and Hindley. The couple asked the young girl to help with carrying their shopping to their car, after dropping it in front of her and then, later, into their house in Wardle Brook Avenue in Hattersley. Once inside Number 16, Lesley Ann was undressed and gagged before being made to pose for pornographic photographs. She was eventually raped and killed and her body buried in a shallow grave on the moor.

Ten months later, Brady picked up 17-year-old Edward Evans at the railway station in Manchester. That night, he was beaten to death with an axe handle. The events surrounding Edward's death were witnessed by Hindley's brother-in-law, David Smith. He reported what he had seen to police. This led to Brady's arrest, and the arrest of Hindley after John Kilbride's name was found scribbled in a notebook at the couple's home along with photographs of the Moor. Police also found a suitcase at the railway station containing the pornographic photos of Lesley Ann and a 13-minute tape of the girl begging for her life. Lesley Ann's body was found first, through analysis of the photos of the moor.

At their trial in 1966, Brady was found guilty of the murders of Lesley Ann, John and Edward. Hindley was found guilty of the murders of Lesley Ann and Edward.

In 1985, Brady and Hindley confessed to the murders of Keith and Pauline. Hindley made two visits to help police find the bodies in 1985 and 1987. Police continued to search and, in July 1987, Pauline's body was found just 100 yards from where Lesley Ann had been discovered in the 1960s. Hindley died in 2002, at the age of 60.

Keith Bennett's body has never been found, much to the heartbreak of his mother, who died in 2012.

In 2013, Brady confessed to the murders of three men and a woman. Since then, in February 2017, Brady hinted that a shotgun, which was found in 2016 near to where he believed he buried Keith Bennett, was one of his 'secret arsenal'. The Eibar double-barrelled shotgun was found wrapped in a sheet under an oak tree on Saddleworth Moor.

Brady died in May 2017, aged 79, at a secure mental health hospital, having spent more than five decades behind bars and having been on hunger strikes since the late 1990s.

Brady never revealed the location of Keith Bennett's grave.

# Henry Lee Lucas and Ottis Toole

The tale of how two men formed what has been called a "homosexual crime team" and embarked on a cross-country murder spree.

**Ottis Toole grew up with his mother who was an abusive religious fanatic. He was sexually abused as a young child by a number of family members, including his older sister, and a neighbour. His mother dressed him in girls's clothes and called him Susan. He was diagnosed in later life as suffering from mental disability.**

As a result of his dysfunctional home life, Toole (born in Jacksonville, Florida in the US in 1947) often ran away and discovered he was sexually aroused by fire – he became an adept arsonist. Meanwhile, Henry Lee Lucas, from Virginia, born 11 years earlier than Toole, became known as America's most prolific serial killer. His life at home was as equally dysfunctional, and he was regularly beaten by his mother, Viola, who on one occasion, beat him so badly he was left in a coma for three days. He was forced to watch his mother having sex with men and, like Toole, was often dressed in girls's clothing. At the age of 10, he was accidentally stabbed in the eye by his brother. The injury was ignored by his mother for four days and his eye was subsequently replaced with a glass eye, which gave him much cause for embarrassment.

The two men met at a Jacksonville soup kitchen in 1976 and entered into a sexual relationship. Seven years later, Toole was arrested for arson while two months after that Lucas was arrested for unlawful possession of a firearm. While in custody, Lucas began to boast about the killing spree that the two men had instigated. Eventually, Toole confessed to the murder of Adam Walsh, aged six, in 1981, two years before their arrests. He was then found guilty of the murder of George Sonnenberg, 64, in 1982, and he was sentenced to death two years later. He was also found guilty of the murder of Silvia Rogers, 19, and received a second death sentence. Both sentences were eventually changed to life sentences on appeal. Lucas committed his first murder in 1960 when he accidentally killed his mother in an argument. He fled the scene, but was sentenced to up to 40 years imprisonment for second-degree murder, despite his protestations that he had acted in self-defence. He was released 10 years later due to prison overcrowding. He drifted around the United States before meeting Toole. By 1978, the two men had set up a homosexual crime team. It appears that Lucas was the main instigator of the murders in which Toole assisted. He eventually confessed to more than 3,000 murders, after his arrest in June 1993. He was convicted of 11 murders and sentenced to the death penalty, which was later commuted to life in prison.

Toole died in prison from liver disease in September 1996. Lucas died of heart failure in prison in 2001.

*ABOVE: Henry Lee Lucas sits in his cell on Texas Death Row in April 1997*

# William Burke and William Hare

The "Burke and Hare murders", also known as the "West Port Murders", were a series of killings in Edinburgh, Scotland, in 1828.

**Lasting for a period of 10 months, the duo lured a total of 16 victims to their deaths from which they profited by selling the corpses to Dr Robert Knox.**

Medical science was blooming and the bodies of executed criminals were considered to be a legitimate source for anatomical study but, with execution rates decreasing, cadavers were in short supply leading to a rise in body snatching; an illegal trade that medical institutions relied upon.

William Burke was born 1792 in Urney in the north of Ireland and emigrated to Scotland in 1817. In earlier life, he dabbled in a variety of trades including serving as an officer's servant in the Donegal militia. William Hare was born in either 1792 or 1804 in Derry or Poyntzpass, Ulster, Ireland, and also emigrated to Scotland, where the pair would eventually meet.

Burke and Hare first became acquainted in 1827 when both men moved into Tanners Close, where Hare's wife ran a lodging house for vagrants. It was on 29th November 1827, that a tenant of the lodging house died of natural causes that presented an opportunity for Hare to recoup the tenant's unpaid rent of £4. The old military pensioner was sold to an assistant of Dr. Robert Knox for £7.10s, while they filled the pensioner's coffin with bark as a means of replicating the man's body weight. After realising the potential profit that could be made, Burke and Hare went on to find more victims.

Their first murder victim was a sick tenant of the lodging house named Joseph whom they plied with alcohol and then suffocated. Burke would hold the arms and legs of the victim down using his legs and elbows and would push the victims head back while covering their nose and mouth. This would ultimately become their favoured method as it left no sign of a struggle on the body of the victim. This technique later became known as the "Burking" method.

When sickly tenants became scarce, the pair began hunting the streets. A further 15 victims were subjected to Burke and Hare's cadaver trade, including an elderly woman and her 12-year-old mute grandson. The pair's dirty trade became unstuck after murdering their final victim, Mary Docherty. When returning lodgers James and Ann Gray discovered the body beneath the bed of a room they had previously stayed in, Burke's mistress, Helen McDougal, tried to bribe the couple, but to no avail.

The police were informed and the investigation began, with Hare being given the opportunity to receive immunity from prosecution if he testified against Burke. On 28th January 1829, Burke received the death penalty by hanging after which he was dissected publically while Hare lived out his life in an undisclosed location.

*BELOW: Helen McDougal, William Burke and William Hare*

# Index/Picture Credits

All images are courtesy of Getty Images with the exception of those from:

• Associated Press (page 40)

• Corbis Images (pages 58, 69, 86, 93, 94, 96, 98, 99, 102, 113, 145, 155, 160)

• Rex Features (pages 10, 11 top, 31, 43, 56, 60, 64, 65, 112, 132, 135, 162, 163, 166, 167)

• Thinkstock (pages 12, 32, 33)

• WikiCommons (pages 57, 77, 109, 126)

• Alamy Stock Photo (pages 37, 136, 137)

# WANTED

SAN FRANCISCO POLICE DEPARTMENT

No. 90-69       WANTED FOR MURDER       OCTOBER 18, 1969

Supplementing our Bulletin 87-69 of October 13, 1969. Additional information has developed the above amended drawing of murder suspect known as "ZODIAC".

WMA, 35-45 Years, approximately 5'8", Heavy Build, Short Brown Hair, possibly with Red Tint, Wears Glasses. Armed with a 9 mm Automatic.

Available for Comparison: Slugs, Casings, Latents, Handwriting.

ANY INFORMATION:
Inspectors Armstrong & Toschi
Homicide Detail
CASE NO. 696314